SIMON & SCHUSTER
CROSSWORD TREASURY

Series 42

Edited by JOHN M. SAMSON

A Fireside Book
Published by Simon & Schuster
New York   London   Toronto   Sydney

FIRESIDE
Rockefeller Center
1230 Avenue of the Americas
New York, NY 10020

For information about special discounts for bulk purchases,
please contact Simon & Schuster Special Sales at
1-800-456-6798 or business@simonandschuster.com

Designed by Sam Bellotto Jr.

Manufactured in the United States of America

10 9 8 7 6 5 4 3 2 1

ISBN-13: 978-0-7432-7056-4

ISBN-10:   0-7432-7056-8

COMPLETE ANSWERS WILL BE FOUND AT THE BACK.

FOREWORD

The Crossword Treasury series continues to attract multitudes of fans who enjoy playing the world's favorite word game.

Selected from earlier editions of the regular series that started it all back in 1924, these crosswords were constructed by the experts for your special entertainment.

Happy puzzling to all!

THE PUBLISHER

IF YOU ENJOY OUR PUZZLES, HERE'S MORE TO EXPLORE.

Simon & Schuster has been publishing outstanding crossword puzzle books every year since 1924—a grand tradition that continues into the twenty-first century.

The world's first and longest-running crossword series continues its tradition of all brand-new and totally original puzzles, constructed by top experts in the field. Editor John M. Samson promises another year of prime cruciverbal wizardry that will keep your brow furrowed and your mind spinning.

So get out your pens or pencils, sharpen your wits, and get ready for months of brain-teasing fun!

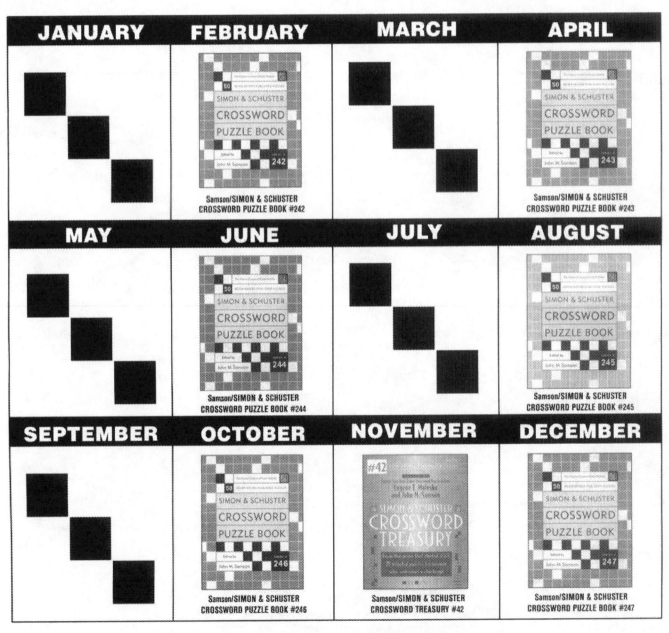

JANUARY FEBRUARY MARCH APRIL

Samson/SIMON & SCHUSTER
CROSSWORD PUZZLE BOOK #242

Samson/SIMON & SCHUSTER
CROSSWORD PUZZLE BOOK #243

MAY JUNE JULY AUGUST

Samson/SIMON & SCHUSTER
CROSSWORD PUZZLE BOOK #244

Samson/SIMON & SCHUSTER
CROSSWORD PUZZLE BOOK #245

SEPTEMBER OCTOBER NOVEMBER DECEMBER

Samson/SIMON & SCHUSTER
CROSSWORD PUZZLE BOOK #246

Samson/SIMON & SCHUSTER
CROSSWORD TREASURY #42

Samson/SIMON & SCHUSTER
CROSSWORD PUZZLE BOOK #247

For Simon & Schuster's online crosswords,
visit us at www.simonsays.com.

1 HIDE AND SEEK by Sam Bellotto Jr.
We lead off with a remarkable construction by a master.

ACROSS

1 "Blondie" character
5 Disco dancer
9 Before card or cream
13 Very cold
14 City N of San Francisco
16 "Talking Vietnam" singer
17 Say 'ere or 'ead
18 "In the guise of ___": Cervantes
19 Orang-___ (ape)
20 Where's Rita?
22 Place of TV
24 TV listing abbr.
25 Mrs. Mahler
26 Former Spanish dollar
27 Sicilian sightseer
29 Fast Eddie's stick
30 Former Davis Cup coach
32 Harvesting machine
34 Closes down
38 Woodstock wear
41 Informed about
42 A1 Mundy's boss
43 Pastry chef's assistant
44 Soccer shots
46 Rock pigeon
47 Bottom line
48 Work after a computer crash
49 It was freed in 1991
51 Kennel command
52 "Let's have a dance ___ are married": Shak.
54 Paid with plastic
55 Andy Capp's order
57 Part of S&L
60 Of the '50s or the '60s
63 Kind of processor
64 Evasive maneuver
67 Where some Chicanos live
68 Where's Bobby?
70 Astrophysicist Penzias
71 Surfer babe
73 Croesus conquest
74 It's as good as a mile
75 Guenon monkey

76 He's Agent 86
77 "Phase IV" foe
78 Short lines?
79 Courtney Love's band

DOWN

1 One in the limelight
2 A.L. Rookie of the Year: 1964
3 First woman in space
4 West German chancellor: 1949–63
5 "___ terror to me": Job 31:23
6 Pizzeria essential
7 Actress in "Klute"
8 Mexican tribe
9 Where's Campbell?
10 Fox or Coyote
11 Climax of many action flicks
12 Crossword laborer
13 Exploit
14 First name in modeling
15 Where's Mrs. Dithers?
21 100 cts.
23 Shaq's alma mater
26 Lightweight velvet
27 Where's Arthur?
28 Where's Tony?
30 Cravat's cousin
31 "The Liner ___ Lady": Kipling
33 To be, in French class
35 Herman's Hermit
36 Patron saint of Wales
37 Flushing field
38 Personal quirks
39 Where's Sally?
40 Crystal gazer

45 "Let's Make ___!"
50 Like an apple-polisher
53 Lady Mountbatten et al.
56 "Love Story" composer
58 Scandinavian and Nova Scotia
59 Kitchen scrap
60 "Splish Splash" singer
61 Steinbeck's middle name
62 Light ___ (feathery)
64 Pertaining to 14609, for instance
65 "Bird on ___": (1990)
66 British mosquito
67 Crimson Tide, for short
68 Trig ratio
69 Major-___
72 DDE predecessor

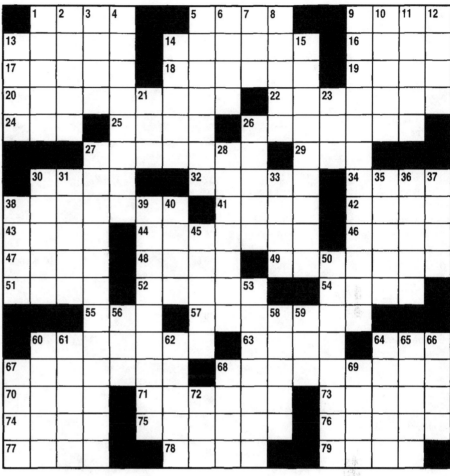

2 GO WEST by Kenneth Haxton
Seasoned travelers should get this one easily.

ACROSS

1 Attendants: Abbr.
6 Mother-in-law of Ruth
11 Italian sauce
16 Fuel additive for racers
17 Actor Booth
18 On the qui vive
19 "___ a Grecian Urn": Keats
20 RHODE ISLAND
22 MASSACHU-SETTS
24 "Sailing" singer
25 Sea east of the Caspian
26 Outplays at bridge
27 Merit
31 NORTH DAKOTA
34 Emulate Anatole France
36 Boat-racer Wood
37 Beverage for Falstaff
38 Official proceedings
40 NEW MEXICO
42 Respond to stimuli
45 Art Deco designer
47 Brian of rock
48 KANSAS
50 INDIANA
55 It docked with Atlantis
56 Source of poi
58 Jellied substance
59 FLORIDA
63 Hecht and Hogan
65 Goof
66 Sass
67 Descriptive word
69 SOUTH CAROLINA
72 Doyle specialty
74 Unit of force
75 Therefore
76 Collect
78 NEW HAMPSHIRE
82 ALABAMA
87 Beaverlike
88 Promotes
89 "The Cocktail Party" dramatist
90 Strainer
91 Beethoven or Spohr opus
92 Oozing with water
93 Weapons for Ko-Ko

DOWN

1 Most quoted author
2 Team
3 Mulligan, for one
4 Pushkin biographer
5 NW Mexican state
6 Wearing a lavaliere
7 Excitement
8 Possess
9 One who affects elegance
10 Torpor
11 O'Brien and Nixon
12 Beethoven dedicatee
13 Wine designation
14 Vehicle for Robert Morse
15 Baseball Hall-of-Famer
21 Leather flask
23 Rajah's missus
26 What Ruth was king of
28 Have ___ at (try)
29 Japanese "King Lear" film
30 FDR org.
31 Painter Chagall
32 Ersatz spread
33 "Hud" actress
35 United, to Brandt
39 Race in the Hambletonian
41 Region
43 Rooster adornment
44 Pilot
46 Wexford locale
49 Philip II's fleets
51 Long life
52 Designer Cassini
53 Yesterday, to Giotto
54 Vaccines
57 Up to it
59 Matterhorn
60 Mae West role
61 Mil. address
62 Unfathomable things
64 Desiccated
68 Preserve fodder
70 Grimm witch
71 Literary Nobelist Rolland
73 Smattering
77 Use an atomizer
79 Double curve
80 Granular snow
81 Bien preceder
82 British Isle
83 Nigerian tribesman
84 Wherewithal in Kobe
85 "Honey ___": Beatles
86 Weasel sound

3 DIZZY DELIGHT   by Robert Zimmerman
Give it a whirl!

ACROSS

1 Cochise, for one
7 ___ and desist
12 British gun
16 Thingamajig
17 Light-bulb gas
18 Up, up and ___
19 Midway spinner
21 Comedian Rudner
22 Wall Street inits.
23 Withdraw
24 Rainbows
26 Nicholas II, e.g.
28 Kind of intersection
29 1930's water project
30 ___ la la
31 Muslim ruler
34 "In the ___": Presley hit
36 Apostatize
38 According to
39 Bulgarian capital
42 Stumble
43 Mobile lead-in
44 Newts
45 Pro vote
46 Musical spinner
50 ___ and gown
51 Savvy
53 Redact
54 Records
56 Gateway
58 Capitol Hill VIP
59 Cartoon canine
60 Shows a response
62 Anxiety
63 Pierre's friend
65 ___ Palmas
66 Grand ___, NS
67 Units of work
71 World Cup sport
73 Trojan hero
76 Before
77 Divan
78 Ceramics spinner
81 Historic periods
82 Turn outward
83 Of the ankle
84 Pavilion
85 "Goodbye, Mr. Chips" star
86 Beginnings

DOWN

1 Fess up
2 "Dead ___ Society" (1989)
3 Cardiologist's concern
4 Naval off.
5 "Airplane!" star
6 Rim
7 Teaching, for one
8 Wear away
9 Malaria symptom
10 Heir
11 Salad plant
12 Rani's robe
13 It's near a bottleneck
14 Diner
15 Large African lake
20 Snow White and friends
25 Squeals
27 Huck Finn's craft
29 Pulsate
32 Tournament
33 Light tan
34 Reach
35 Digit
36 Israeli general
37 Summer spinner
38 Insert
40 Topograph-ical boot
41 Vipers
42 What's in store
43 El Misti locale
47 Reposes
48 Singer k.d.
49 Space chimp
52 Three, in Trieste
55 Semiquaver, for one
57 Ivy League campus
59 Look scornfully
61 Complained
62 Peter of TV news
63 Black-ink item
64 "Bed and Breakfast" star
66 City of ancient Arabia
68 Ebbets Field infielder
69 "___ Expectations"
70 Peddles
72 Playbill listing
73 Solar disk
74 Concerning
75 Balletomane's lake
79 Ab ___ (from the beginning)
80 Ruth's 714: Abbr.

4 SPORTS BAG by Sam Bellotto Jr.
Sam found these curious facts in the Information Please Almanac.

ACROSS

1 Herod the Great's realm
6 Decides on
10 Use a rotoscope
15 Secretary of the Interior: 1961–69
16 Sarge's superior
18 Of a branch
19 Not greater than 250 feet per second
22 Clytemnestra's mother
23 Thickness measurer
24 More cozy
27 "The Lawnmower ___" (1992)
28 Third degree?
29 East Indian liquor
30 Belief
32 Actress Zetterling
33 Milkcap game
36 Exactly 120 feet long by 60 feet wide
41 Jeff Sluman's org.
42 Life in a UFO
43 "___ to leap tall buildings . . ."
44 Telamon's ship
45 Seafarer
47 Slow train
49 Frodo's foe
50 Liquidate
52 Luminary
53 Earth ending
55 Mother's Day present?
58 Precisely 127 feet and 3-3/8 inches
62 TV chef
63 Sportscaster Berman
64 North of NY
65 N Carolina motto opener
66 Quaff for Capt. Picard
67 Immature newt
69 They're usually boring
71 Suite sharer
74 ICBM container
75 Not more than 60 inches from heel to end of shaft
80 Like some breakfast cereals
81 City on the Red River
82 Dressed to the ___
83 His portrait is worth $50
84 "Watch your ___!"
85 Ridicule

DOWN

1 Corn-liquor container
2 Japanese salad plant
3 ___ segno
4 Like Yoda
5 "Three Tall Women" playwright
6 Earthen pot
7 Officeholder
8 Puccini's Floria
9 Jewish month
10 Of nutrition
11 Hied
12 Mideast millionaire
13 Jellicle Ball attendees
14 English cathedral town
17 Carapo
20 Lost in space
21 Digestive enzyme
24 Hardware on a barn door
25 Part of OEM
26 Seaport in W Mexico
27 Marseilles Mrs.
31 English cheese
32 Thousand squared
33 Buy
34 Part of NOW
35 Ronnie & The Daytonas hit
37 "___ the land of the free . . ."
38 Mother-of-pearl
39 Olajuwon's org.
40 Trireme puller
46 Covergirl Carol
48 Rio Treaty implementer
49 Fort near Monterey
50 "Tinker, Tailor, Soldier, ___"
51 She, in Lisbon
52 Erotic
54 Open the door to
56 Former GDR ally
57 Leggy pair
59 Tungsten, e.g.
60 Pallet
61 Showy houseplant
66 Straphanger's fare
67 Kett and James
68 Deceptive maneuver
70 Suffix for corp
71 Bestial bellow
72 Eight: Comb. form
73 Timber tree
74 Cut class
75 Glutton
76 George in "Blind Date"
77 Lion's prey
78 Number of toes on a chimpanzee
79 FDR's successor

5 NATIONAL DEBT   by Fran and Lou Sabin
Our native tongue owes a lot to influences from abroad.

ACROSS

1 Cobra's cousin
6 Discomfit
11 Actress Belafonte
16 Liquid portion of fat
17 Distance runner Waitz
18 Kind of institution
19 "Beat it!"
21 Clarinetist Shaw
22 Covent Garden melody
23 Overtrump
24 Create a recess
25 Computer cabinet
28 Fashion designer Paloma
30 Emulate Picabo Street
31 Brown wall cover?
33 Pick, pick, pick
34 Steelie's target
37 On, and on, and on . . .
41 Woo
44 Nav. reading
45 Whiting
47 Hamburger helper
48 Disinclined
51 "The Thames" painter
52 Lane in "Knight Moves"
53 Formal mall
54 The best
55 Catcher
56 Worked out, in a way
58 Yale, to Elis
63 Pro ___
64 Hosp. areas
66 "Shut your ___!"
67 Delicious, at a luau
68 Julie in "That's Life!"
72 Hold capacity
75 Buzzy place
77 Romano source
79 Souvanna Phouma ruled here
80 Charlotte ___ (dessert)
81 Unlimited
85 Wahine ta-ta
86 Small Persian rug

87 Battle zone
88 Stripped, in a way
89 Prepare challah
90 City on the Meuse

DOWN

1 Extinct ratite
2 Free-for-___
3 Skin color factor
4 Sepulchers
5 WW2 beachhead
6 Of yore
7 Vintner's adjective
8 "The Fox and the Grapes" author
9 Intervene
10 Mother lobster
11 Crosses
12 Large groups
13 Before everything
14 Sadie Thompson's story
15 "___ a song . . ."
20 Traveling bag
24 Jafar's parrot
25 Clay's org.
26 Rubber-stamped
27 Poetic dusk
29 Sign of something missing
32 Rowdy type
35 Windows symbol
36 Molto ___
38 Fall bloom
39 Poe house
40 Devilfish
42 Computer adjunct
43 Novelist Brookner
46 Jazz-pop singer Smith
48 Hang tough
49 Leather flask
50 Home-style
51 La familia member
55 Campania seaport

57 Like "Alien"
59 Tumbler's surface
60 Said "Prosit!"
61 Sheffield loc.
62 Pitching Preacher
65 Neutral nation of WW2
69 "The Unfortunate Traveler" author
70 Consternation
71 Lowlife
73 Waif watchers
74 Pointe-___, Congo
75 Composer Khachaturian
76 Hungarian dog
78 Resort SE of Palermo
81 Show curiosity
82 It's "in"
83 Merkel in "A Tiger Walks"
84 Homo sapiens

MUSIC, MAESTRO!   by Nancy Scandrett Ross
This puzzle's subject was a member of Italy's first Parliament.

ACROSS

1 Grouch
5 Colorful shrub in autumn
10 Blandly urbane
15 Farm machinery pioneer
16 School subj.
17 John Osborne emotion
18 Opera by 13 Down
21 Penultimate opera by 13 Down
22 First scene of 21 Across
23 No ifs, ___ or buts
24 Seville sun
25 Korean soldiers
27 He always gets his man
29 Lou Grant's paper
31 Bertie Wooster expletive
32 Opera by 13 Down
38 "Flesh and Bone" actress
41 Inborn
42 Slippery customers
43 Mercutio's subject
45 Husbander
46 Move about restlessly
47 Filmed anew
50 Perfect number
51 Leo's tresses
52 Jubilant
53 Depend
56 Opera by 13 Down
58 Kernel bearers
60 M. Descartes
61 Devilfish
64 Tai tongue
66 It goes before the "carte"
69 French cathedral city
70 "___ Men": Porter
72 Tailor's insert
75 Opera by 13 Down
78 Harden
79 Positive thinker
80 "Call Me ___" (1953)
81 Attempt
82 Equip
83 Affirmatives

DOWN

1 Hundred, to 13 Down
2 Defiant one
3 Sea east of the Caspian
4 Chime
5 ___ Miguel
6 Brownie of Scottish folklore
7 After-dinner treats
8 Air: Comb. form
9 Alluring ones
10 Arm of the USAF
11 Manually inept
12 Deputy
13 "Oberto" was his first
14 Rub out
15 Couples
19 Longtime "Saturday Evening Post" editor
20 Urban pollution
26 Sash for Cio-Cio-San
28 Former Mideast org.
29 Ivan or Boris
30 Appraise
32 Koko had a "little" one
33 ___ den Linden
34 "___ ear and out . . ."
35 Over 18
36 Inclined, in London
37 Senior
39 Baritone Pasquale
40 Consumer advocate
44 Eliot's Adam
47 This leads to tragedy in 56 Across
48 Dash
49 Win at chess
51 Deform
54 Heroine of 75 Across
55 Terrier's bark
57 Mouths
59 Role in 56 Across
61 Tillstrom puppet
62 Printer's inks
63 Vegetarian choices
64 Place
65 "___, Ma Baby"
66 Stage comment
67 Home and Olin
68 Speck
71 Yemen capital
73 West Point monogram
74 Collar stiffener
76 Juan Carlos, e.g.
77 Morning moisture

7 METEOROLOGICAL   by Wilson McBeath
The barometer starts falling after 19 Across.

ACROSS
1 Part of a procedure
5 Prospectors' pack animals
11 Lathers
16 Dot on the Ebro
17 Bonkers
18 Bronze Roman coin
19 He's no bosom buddy
22 Wall Street denizens
23 Kind of ticket
24 Stannum
25 S Netherlands city
26 Serving well
28 Wash
29 Meager
32 City near the French-Belgian border
33 Destiny deities
34 Electrolysis atoms
35 Tea type
36 Surgeon General in 1994
37 Almond
38 Apples and pears
39 Suit to ___
40 Upstages
46 Make progress
47 Provide provender
48 Fire
49 Guile
52 Pertaining to the cheek
53 Olive ___
54 Cousin of an oribi
55 More faint
56 Abounds
57 Pitcher Blyleven
58 Soras
59 Earth's star
60 Old capital of Burma
61 Ex-Packer Starr
62 Some are dire
66 Puts in an IRA
70 Day's march
71 Pope's representative
72 Dash
73 Patron saint of France
74 "My Cup Runneth Over" singer
75 Take-out order

DOWN
1 Examine closely
2 Industrial giant
3 Lamb
4 Gubernatorial absolutions
5 Oktoberfest quaffs
6 Merkel and O'Connor
7 Q–U connection
8 Rally yell
9 1760 yards
10 Composed
11 Roll and bind
12 Naval CIA
13 Synthetic fabric
14 1942 Garson role
15 Melancholy
20 "I'm No Angel" star
21 Tire
26 "Silent Snow, Secret Snow" author
27 Squeaker
28 Oppressed
29 Roosts
30 Prince Albert, for one
31 Poet Bradstreet
32 Negus ingredient
33 Boulogne bloom
35 Assume as a fact
36 Diethyl oxide
38 Inverness garb
39 Perfume
41 Ten-percenter
42 Kind of tax
43 Bell the cat
44 Midterm
45 Stonewall's soldiers
49 Vitiated
50 Elate
51 Camelback group
52 Headwaiter
53 Procrastinated
55 Inmate's hope
56 Rip in "Cross Creek"
58 WW2 heroes
59 Pigs' digs
61 Educational degrees
62 Cloy
63 Run in neutral
64 Luzon volcano
65 Since, to Burns
67 Finial
68 Turkish title
69 Southdown male

8 LOCATION, LOCATION by Mary E. Brindamour
A unique placement exam from our Bay State teacher.

ACROSS

1 Hawkeye
6 Thick slice
10 Take a gift
16 Shout of approval
17 Tide's partner
18 Skullcap
19 Go by car
20 O
22 Tips
24 "Les Misérables" novelist
25 Curves
26 Rainy mo.
28 More frigid
30 Out ___ limb
33 Shoe width
34 Marred
36 Accented
39 Doc Holliday's friend
40 Signal approval
42 1970 World's Fair site
43 "Little ___ of Horrors" (1986)
44 Crockett's last stand
46 Expunge
50 Credo
52 Struck sharply
54 Ring boundaries
55 Involve
57 Dr. Salk's target
59 ___ libre (free verse)
60 Kind of drum
62 Faberge jeweled this
63 "The King and I" heroine
64 Pittsburgh eleven
67 Grapevine item
69 Golf score
70 It runs in Vermont
71 Sweetened the pot
73 Librarian degree
74 Blackthorn fruit
76 Little bit
78 Mediocre
80 Y
84 Shares rides
87 Mideastern princes
88 Shamu, for one
89 Innsbruck locale
90 Has the most smarts
91 Bullrush
92 Teen magazine

DOWN

1 Big Blue
2 Spanish gold
3 W
4 Bath's river
5 Scandinavian
6 Wall and Main
7 Supple
8 Love affairs
9 Titanic sinker
10 Network monogram
11 Fair grade
12 Miracle site
13 Main course
14 Made a quilt
15 Succinct
21 Anchors
23 Elaborate aria
26 "___ Fideles"
27 Female pheasant
29 Sacred cows
31 At hand
32 Cross-examiner
35 Make concessions
37 Play the flute
38 Russian urn
41 Flue adjunct
45 Bossy remark
47 D
48 Occuring in the spring
49 Elia's output
51 Fork features
53 Black pool ball
56 After ooh or tra
58 Curved arches
61 Fasten again
64 Deli specialty
65 Figures of speech
66 Form of irony
68 Takes as one's own
69 Horsefeathers!
72 John ___ Garner
75 Olympic sword
77 Olfactory stimulant
79 Brown sauce
81 They make cents
82 "Dulce et decorum ___": Horace
83 Traipse
85 Angeles lead-in
86 Stallone

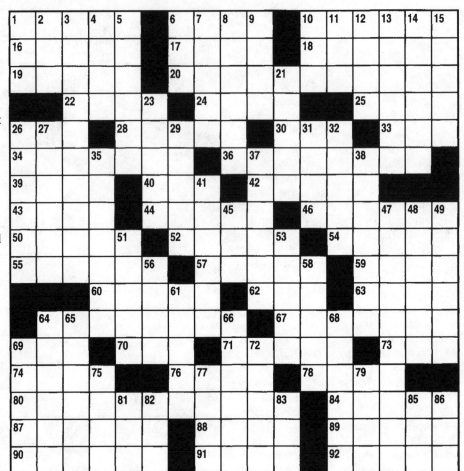

9 TRAVELING BANDS   by Randall J. Hartman

This puzzle gives new meaning to the hit "Band on the Run."

ACROSS

1 "Apollo 13" actor
7 Tony Gwynn's tool
10 Setup man
15 "Begone!"
16 Stage direction
17 Weird
18 Rock group featuring Grace Slick
21 Comparison words
22 Other
23 Mends
24 Eden, e.g.
27 Mine passage
28 ___ and the Continental Kids ("American Graffiti")
32 United
35 "___ the Walrus": Beatles
36 Moray
37 Broadcast
38 Saga
39 Shock
41 Apron part
42 "The Sound of ___"
43 "Brown-Eyed Girl" singer
47 Head bee
50 Wash. neighbor
51 Warehouses
55 Forearm bone
56 Genetic initials
57 L–P connection
58 Diamonds
59 Not safe
60 "Ridin' the Storm Out" group
64 Clan
65 Under control
66 Goddess of wisdom
69 Rabbit tail
70 Killer whale
74 "We're an American Band" group
78 Awaken
79 Cleo's river
80 Sewing necessity
81 "A House Is Not a Home" author
82 Nice summer
83 Determine

DOWN

1 Moslem pilgrim
2 Streets
3 Huck Finn's transport
4 Light orange
5 Chemical suffix
6 Orch. section
7 Dwarf tree
8 Wings
9 Japanese fish
10 Type of tank
11 Serf
12 Where Tehran is
13 ___ of credit
14 Spike and Harper
16 State of matter
19 Flower part
20 Speed trap
25 Fleming's "___ With the Golden Gun"
26 Indian or Arctic
27 Defendant's story
28 Trim
29 Burmese gibbon
30 Japanese diver
31 Simba's den
32 Used to be
33 Yale student
34 Winter mo.
38 Fish from a can
40 Ocular layer
41 Howard Hughes designed one
42 Detroit's moniker
44 North Dakota city
45 Harem rooms
46 ___ message
47 "___ Vadis" (1951)
48 Inuit tool
49 Type of Dr.
52 Male chauvinist ___
53 "Travels in Hyperreality" author
54 D.C. figure
56 Coffee preference
57 Conductor from Bombay
60 Present
61 Hamburger topper
62 Harden
63 Idolizes
64 Feeling
66 Pearl Mosque site
67 Walked
68 Tote
69 Tiff
71 Took the bus
72 Ripken and Thomas
73 Summer coolers
75 One, in France
76 Once ___ lifetime
77 "___ Miserables"

ACROSS

1 Capone's nemesis
5 Ruth's beloved
9 Shelley and
  Swinburne
15 Battle of the ___
16 Angry reaction
17 Tempest site
18 **Words of wisdom
  by 61 Across**
21 Fireworks paths
22 Invisible fluid?
23 Fleur-de-___
24 Harris Fox
25 Most theoretical
27 Manipulate dice
28 "Club Dance"
  network
29 **Words of wisdom:
  Part II**
33 Bud holder
34 "___ ole davil,
  sea": O'Neill
36 Kind of general
37 Arboretum
  specimen
39 Diesel-engine sub
41 Fleet bigwig: Abbr.
42 "Pure Country" star
46 **Words of wisdom:
  Part III**
50 Old Faithful, e.g.
51 Sundial hour
52 In a crooked
  position
53 Like the Kalahari
55 Just back from the
  laundry
57 Mime duo?
58 Certain domino
61 Words of wisdom
  source
64 Do voodoo
65 Babylonian deity
66 Having wings
69 Jack in "The
  Villain"
71 Pacers' org.
72 Paul and Peter
74 "Germinal" author
75 **Words of wisdom:
  Part IV**
79 Buck topper
80 Fallen Timbers
  locale
81 "There ___
  losers"
82 Enunciated
83 Nantes
  names
84 Played for a
  sucker

DOWN

1 Gandhi
  associate
2 Abhorrent
3 Perceives
4 Retiree's
  support org.
5 Mash
  ingredient
6 Hoggish
  noise
7 Eruption
  fallout
8 Enthusiast
9 Baseball's
  Mel and Ed
10 ___ volente
11 Poetic foot
12 Laconia's
  capital
13 Turnstile
  unlockers
14 "Tristram
  Shandy"
  author
15 Product exchange
19 Tiny specks
20 Out of ___
26 Illegal pitch
27 Of long duration
30 Fix permanently
31 "What ___ say?"
32 Highlands tongue
33 Zorina and Miles
34 Alphabetic
  foursome
35 Rose's beau
38 Fuel additive
40 Try out
43 Requested an
  audience
44 Gossip column
  squib
45 Wreckers
47 Advanced math
48 26.418 gallons
49 Went quickly

54 Mrs. Fields
56 Pull ___ one (cheat)
58 Bara and
  namesakes
59 Ease off
60 Track bet
62 Lucidity
63 "The ___ edge"
67 Serengeti roamer
68 "The Banana Boat
  Song"
70 Cartoonist Caniff
71 Dweeb
72 Leveling stick
73 New Mexican
  resort
76 "A Summer Place"
  star
77 Elliott Gould film
78 Sigma follower

SING! SING! SING!   by Bob Sefick
We have only one word to say about this: Good! Good! Good!

ACROSS

1 ___ noche (tonight)
5 Stimpy, for one
8 Attacked on the fly
15 Caper
16 Peer Gynt's mater
17 That's the size of it
18 Bobby Rydell hit
20 Cornice brackets
21 Gawky
22 Unguis
23 Upset
24 "___ so it goes . . ."
25 On the crest
26 Take off
28 Halsey's outfit: Abbr.
31 Tree ornaments
33 Encounters
35 Le Havre household
36 Speaker at Cooperstown
38 Gone ___ (out of shape)
39 Con's ropes?
42 Zap
43 Is in the past
46 Jo Jo Gunne hit
48 Composer Rorem
49 "___ Old Cowhand"
51 Hammered
53 "Down low" shot
55 Sugary suffixes
56 Seat vacater
60 Lack of faith
62 Standing
63 Bibliophile's collection
64 Change for a five
65 Bay in SW Oregon
66 W.S. Gilbert's nom de plume
67 Itches
69 Hit the road
70 "___ Grand Night for Singing"
71 Ropes
74 Bill Cosby hit
76 Non-movers
77 Wish away
78 French painter Jules ___

79 Senior member
80 California fort
81 Unlocks poetically

DOWN

1 Highlight
2 Sub
3 Timely sound
4 Hamburg head-slapper
5 Brazilian exports
6 Equally sharp
7 Bluish shade
8 Little, for Burns
9 "One man with a mind can beat ___ who haven't": Shaw
10 Most suggestive
11 ___ now (to date)
12 The Beach Boys hit
13 Palindromic preposition
14 ___ Plaines
15 See 29 Down
19 Chipped in
25 "Tattered Tom" author
26 Courtney Cox show
27 Glisten, in London
29 Demand one's due, with 15 Down
30 Observed
32 Semi section
34 Positive particle
36 D'Artagnan's moves
37 Gather once more
40 Powdery tobacco
41 Sauna state
43 Pebbles' role model
44 Forcefully

45 McCartney-Jackson hit
47 Charles and Ephron
50 Loony tune
52 Picker's pittance
54 You or me
57 Secondary classification
58 They rub the wrong away
59 Change headquarters
61 Not spotted
62 In the bag
65 ___ d'Alene
68 Italian fortress town
69 Rookie
70 "The time ___!"
71 Dangerous drug
72 From ___ Z
73 Mariner's hdg.
75 Tokyo of old

12 A LITTLE FISHY by Arthur S. Verdesca
How many denizens of the deep can you find below?

ACROSS

1 Soft cap
6 Ancient Egyptian symbol
12 Cries of triumph
16 Eat away
17 El Greco's city
18 Peace Nobelist: 1946
19 Last heir
21 Besides
22 Bisected fly
23 Commander of the "Schamhorst"
24 Of an epoch
26 Sandburg's "The People, ___"
27 Operate a combine
28 Sourdough's strike
29 "Falcon Crest" star
31 Modern surgical tools
34 "Catriona" auth.
35 Talaria appendage
36 "It ___ little of us here:" Frost
37 Horatian works
39 Kind of lens
42 Deseret, today
43 Special interest group
45 Blamed
47 Bullock film, with "The"
48 Vociferous
50 Conclusion
51 End titles
53 Gull
54 Burns' hillside
55 Designer of the White House
56 Portent
58 Looks like
59 Fort near Monterey
60 Opposed
61 Alpine abode
62 Verbal outpouring
64 Spring mo.
65 Type of dorm
66 Smoke particles
67 Pro ___ (in proportion)
69 Vale
70 Caldron

73 Cotton Blossom captain
75 Type of sculpture
78 Aforementioned
79 Lorraine's companion
80 Modify
81 Nothing, to Diego
82 Smooths
83 Narrow

DOWN

1 Worst, in a way
2 Libido, in psychoanalysis
3 Iago, e.g.
4 Netherlands piano center
5 Mosaic piece
6 Bad bug
7 Bay
8 Clay, today
9 Check or defeat
10 Worship
11 Cold Adriatic wind
12 GP's group
13 Wow!
14 Uncertain
15 German sculptor
20 Arrow poison
25 S.A. ruminants
27 Hebrew letter
28 Eccentric ancient
30 Thicke of TV
31 Catapult
32 Star: Comb. form
33 Rode like Marty McFly
34 Lodge
38 Ward off
40 Change the title
41 Most fantastic
43 Cold sandwich
44 Girl
46 Cry's partner

48 Scoria
49 Pipsqueak
52 Egg and ___
54 Chaplet member
57 Cul-de-sac
58 Trounce
61 "Ramblin' Rose" singer
62 Tint
63 Black-and-white beast
64 For any reason
65 Demeter, to Cicero
68 Down with, in Dijon
69 Join spacecraft
70 Line-item ___
71 Bird class
72 Lacerated
74 Singer Sumac
76 Initials on an oilcan
77 Adverse

13 STATIONER'S SUPPLY   by Frances Hansen
This puzzle's theme was inspired by an office supply cabinet.

ACROSS

1 "From Here to Eternity" role
7 Balanced
12 Hemingway's handle
16 Here and there
17 "As ___ and breathe!"
18 "Jeopardy" host Trebek
19 Web of deceit?
21 Appropriate
22 Owns
23 Satisfy fully
24 Divinely influenced
26 Bagnold
28 Heat measure
30 Untold years
31 Collation
34 Kitchen garbage?
40 Women's org. since 1890
41 Maupassant's "Bel ___"
42 President Grant's first name, originally
43 "___ Mucho": 1944 song
46 Backtalk
48 West Coast wine valley
49 Distinctive time period
50 Diploma?
54 Strauss's "___ Rosenkavalier"
55 Bridle parts
57 ___ Finklea (Cyd Charisse)
58 Apprehend
60 Certain circular windows
62 DeLuise in "Loose Cannons"
63 Kanga's baby
64 Hobbes, in a way?
67 Stabbed
71 Attention
72 Drink for an ant
74 Fashionable beach resort
75 Backpack
80 Boat spar
83 Sydney's state: Abbr.
84 Knotty problems
85 Duplicates
88 Like Nash's "lama"
89 City on the Moselle
90 Tell tales on
91 Scrawny
92 Indian antelope
93 Weigh on

DOWN

1 Cotton or Increase
2 French-built rocket
3 Dish out the dirt
4 Cat in "Cats"
5 "But most it is presumption ___ . . .": Shak.
6 Concert halls
7 TV's "One ___ Live"
8 Building afterthought
9 Shakespeare's "Henry ___"
10 Smooth
11 Abate
12 Mandy of "Impromptu"
13 Winglike
14 Lap dog
15 Gave the heave-ho
20 NY betting letters
25 Swank
27 Arp's movement
29 Feeling no remorse
32 Coarse hominy
33 Trick's alternative
35 Mosque prayer leader
36 Beauvais' department
37 Turkish decree
38 Scruffs
39 Chic
43 '40s jazz
44 Writer Jong
45 Took notice, visibly
47 Boojum
51 Designer Gernreich
52 Dancing shoe
53 Disney film: 1982
56 In a drowsy way
59 Stir up the waters
61 Cleopatra's maid
65 Pamphlets
66 Like one with renewed faith
68 Having limits
69 Detroit duds
70 Probes for water
73 Carried the day
75 Dial
76 Mother's admonition
77 Arabian sea gulf
78 Williams of "Rhoda"
79 Singer Jensen
81 Numerical prefix
82 Son of Lot
86 "___ Mir Bist Du Schoen": Cahn
87 Parts of qts.

14 LIVE AND LEARN   by Alfio Micci
Everyone should agree with the bit of wisdom below.

ACROSS

1 World Series champs: 1990
5 **Author of the quote (with 74 Across)**
10 A.k.a.
15 Type of type
17 Can, in Cannes
18 Latin American dance
19 "The Last ___ Saw Paris"
20 Kinds
21 Leafy trembler
22 **Start of a quote**
25 He was Ernie Bilko
26 1502, to Flavius
27 Soak flax
30 Corner
31 Banned weatherproofer: Abbr.
33 Groan producer
34 Ashen
35 Sore
37 It runs in a taxi
38 Lost traction
42 Declare
43 Receive from
44 **Middle of the quote**
48 Pierce
49 Seed coat
50 Musical Horne
51 City of India
52 Western spread
54 Contemporary of Dashiell
55 Bumped into
56 Islet
58 Ten: Comb. form
62 "De Civitate ___": Augustine
63 Season
64 Love affair
66 **End of the quote**
70 Jane Eyre's pupil
72 Opera highlights
73 Actress Valli
74 **See 5 Across**
75 "That ever I was born to ___ right": Shak.
76 Resign
77 Hen
78 Utopian spots
79 Lavish excessive love on

DOWN

1 Makeup exam
2 Panacea
3 Facial feature
4 Put in the hold
5 Crazed
6 Anon
7 About, briefly
8 Have a go at
9 Ash
10 Stradivari's teacher
11 Whip
12 Preemptory
13 Publisher Hirschfeld
14 Heir
16 Green land
23 George's lyricist
24 Go astray
28 Teatime
29 Diva Stratas
32 Fraternal address
34 Danger
36 Nordic
37 Ryan in "Innerspace"
38 Shot from ambush
39 Monte-mezzi's "___ dei Tre Re"
40 How boors behave
41 Revolutionary hero Silas
42 "___ Maria"
43 Delores ___ Rio
45 Guido's note
46 Killer whale
47 They deny existence
52 PR handout
53 Clad
55 ___ jongg
57 "___ the season . . ."
58 Used an old phone
59 Inuit
60 Redact jointly
61 Having a handle
63 Take the helm
65 Just ___ (not much)
67 Shoppe modifier
68 Ceremony
69 Premier
70 Cobbler's tool
71 Day, in Durango

15 THE MALE ANIMAL by Janet R. Bender
How many creatures can you find hiding in the squares below?

ACROSS

1 Froth
6 Mania
11 Sprayed an attacker
16 Small drum
17 Pitcher Martinez
18 Bakery emanation
19 Worship
20 Farewell, amigo
21 Former Israeli premier
22 Monetary doctrine
24 Like a jumping Jack
25 Fill to excess
26 Social reformer Jacob
27 In one's second childhood
28 Korean border river
30 Witty
31 Police alert
34 Light axes
37 Wall Street regulator
40 Actress Lane of "The Nanny"
42 Injures
43 List ender
44 Filthy riches
45 Surgical beam
46 Plants
47 Poses a question
48 Necessities
49 Knot or glasses
50 Society-page word
51 London and its suburbs
53 Dangerous curve
54 Muse of comedy
56 Load freight
58 Tristram's beloved
59 Hawaiian garlands
61 Romanov bigwig
65 Perfect models
66 Like a condemned building
68 Gets close to
69 Green piece
70 TV's "Evening ___"
71 "Midnight Cowboy" character
72 Type size

73 Heads, in Hyères
74 German industrial city
75 Greek physician
76 Dunne in "Back Street"

DOWN

1 Uses a knife
2 Mantegna's birthplace
3 Metal fastener
4 Safer of "60 Minutes"
5 Part of a famous palindrome
6 Skull
7 Wheel spokes
8 Faulty
9 Camera lens
10 Half-picas
11 QB Dan's family
12 A Musketeer
13 Paving of yore
14 Author Zola
15 Isak Dinesen, e.g.
23 Synthetic fiber
24 Violin parts
27 Farmer, at times
29 To ___ (exactly)
30 Mary Stuart's son
31 Poe's middle name
32 Stop
33 Console neighbors
35 "Seward's Folly"
36 ___ la vista
38 Pulls down
39 Modeling materials
41 Intercity haulers: Abbr.
43 Guido's highest note
45 Desi's daughter
46 Hall-of-Famer Biletnikoff

48 Shapes
49 Grind the teeth
51 Visits briefly
52 Shine
55 Suffering from laryngitis
57 Aquatinter
58 Brainstorms
59 Former French premier
60 Tread the boards
62 Fish or footwear
63 Standish's cabin-mate
64 Witherspoon in "S.F.W."
65 Memo words
66 Baltic city
67 ___ spumante
69 Hammarskjöld

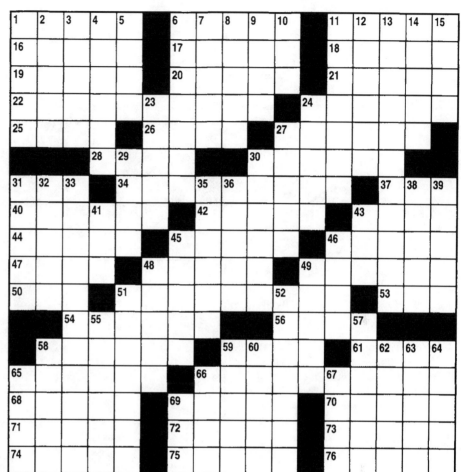

ACROSS

1 Resort near Santa Fe
5 Cornfield cry
8 Funnyman Bill, briefly
11 Baseball's Boggs
15 Culture starter
16 Funhouse sounds
18 Arabian Sea gulf
19 Cheap seats
21 Touch down
22 "___ Laughing" (1967)
23 Ruhr Valley city
24 "Workers of the world ___!"
25 ___ one's own juices
27 Asian New Year
28 Toughened
29 SAT takers
31 Religious pamphlet
33 Kennel comment
36 Moby Dick's pursuer
39 Kitchen-appliance shade
43 On-line letter
45 "The ___ Daba Honeymoon"
46 Jurist Hand
47 Kirov cash
48 Dueler's maneuver
50 Gave up
51 Morgiana's master
53 Part of TGIF
54 Lots and lots
55 Dakar's land
56 Circumnavigator Phileas
58 Flattens
59 Of the hinterland
61 "My dog ___ fleas . . ."
63 Temporary pet-watcher
66 Badminton do-over
69 Scarecrow portrayer
74 Speedy horses
75 "La Belle ___"
77 "After the Bath" painter
78 Clinton Cabinet member
79 Oval
81 Like cuttlefish secretion
82 Rap's ___ Boys
83 "You ___ Me": Cooke
84 Arnaz in "Forever Darling"
85 Computer inserts
86 Bewitch
87 Foster's dog

DOWN

1 Watergate evidence
2 FBI member
3 Emulate Demosthenes
4 Tendon
5 Chi. time
6 Require a rubdown
7 Twist forcefully
8 Talk-show host Dick
9 Augury
10 Job-application info
11 City NE of Oakland
12 Noted firefighter Red
13 Al ___ (pasta preference)
14 Brought to a halt
17 ___ out (get rid of tactfully)
20 "Armageddon" author
24 Remove from a car
26 Gun grp.
28 Icicle locale
30 Clinton cabinet member
32 Favorite of Elizabeth I
33 Stubborn as ___
34 1994 Peace Nobelist
35 Mile record-holder in 1975
37 ___-Simbel
38 Canadian national park
40 Combining form for "male"
41 Monopoly cards
42 Racetrack figures
43 Geologic time periods
44 Golfing groups
49 12 doz.
52 Roseanne, formerly
57 Yak
60 Andean ruminants
62 Jr.-to-be
63 Tasty
64 Ryan of "The Beverly Hillbillies"
65 Sherman and Abrams
67 Love personified
68 Chayefsky's "The ___ Man"
70 Part of LCD
71 Astonished one
72 "Maria ___"
73 "I Am Woman" woman
75 Begged
76 Peter Gunn's love
79 Disney purchase
80 Madonna book

17 HARDY SOULS   by Brad Wilber

A top constructor honors the 70th anniversary of the Hardy Boys.

ACROSS

1 Fleet
6 Stephen King specialty
10 Sweet-milk cheese
14 "Swan Lake" siren
15 Result in
18 "___ Only Just Begun"
19 THE MYSTERY OF THE ___ (book 43)
21 Douay Bible book
22 Radio silence
23 Thugs
25 Draft org.
26 Frequent partner of the Hardys
28 Joe Hardy's steady
29 Ogden Nash's birthplace
30 Retainer
31 Showtime competitor
33 Deer trail
35 Gel containers
38 Chinese dynastic name
40 Feline crossbreed
43 Grand Ole ___
44 "Ionica" poet
45 Synthetic dye
47 Classic car
48 Without discount
50 Candler of Coca-Cola fame
51 Escritoire item
53 Wine prefix
54 "And giving ___, up the chimney . . .": Moore
55 Concert hall
56 Belgrade residents
58 Bishop's hat: Brit.
59 Garden State cagers
61 AAA map abbr.
62 Cicero's voice
63 LAPD call
65 Chili pot
67 The Hardys' best friend
69 Seance reply
72 Polish dance
75 Mesabi Range output
77 Objective
78 THE MYSTERY OF THE ___ (book 45)
80 "Betsy's Wedding" star
81 Mellifluous
82 Maestro John ___ Gardiner
83 Moray's milieu
84 Nolin of "Baywatch"
85 Doltish

DOWN

1 "Country ___" (Denver hit)
2 Steel-headed tools
3 Mideast breads
4 "Where Is the Life That Late ___?"
5 Rosary sets
6 Snowblindness cause
7 "___ a perfumed sea . . .": Poe
8 ___ avis
9 Issue
10 Endor furball
11 MYSTERY OF THE ___ (book 40)
12 Novelist Corman
13 Reagan cabinet member
16 Cowardly Lion harasser
17 Some graduate exams
20 What Wallenda walked
24 Frank Hardy's steady
27 Spin
30 Puckish
32 The Hardys' hometown
34 Friction fighter
35 "Flying Down ___" (1933)
36 Capsize
37 THE CLUE OF THE ___ (book 21)
38 Shows indolence
39 Advances
41 "Scandalized Masks" painter
42 "Hard Cash" author
44 ___-de-sac
46 Cpl., for one
48 The Hardys' dad
49 Early stringed instrument
52 Dolor
54 City N of Marseilles
57 Wipeout maneuvers
58 Went by car
60 Mark down
62 Action word
63 Newborn test
64 John le Carre's birthplace
66 T'ang Dynasty poet
68 Margaret ___ Thatcher
69 "The Age of Bronze" sculptor
70 An enemy of Sparta
71 QB Rodney
73 Patron saint of Norway
74 Part of HOMES
76 Shade of green
79 Of copper: Abbr.

18 LITERARY LAUGHS by Tap Osborn

A pro from the Sunshine State authors some clever puns.

ACROSS

1 Polyester fabric
7 Loathe
12 Fundamentals
16 Do a greenskeeper's job
17 Mixture
18 Polish lancer
19 Emily's monster pet?
21 Register ringer
22 Pittance
23 Niche
24 Wall steps
25 Dine at nine
28 Bernhardt rival
29 Codger
30 Supreme councils
32 They have yens
34 Foreman's assistant
35 Symphony member
36 Revokes legally
37 Factory
38 Fictional captain
42 Iraqi port
43 Goes gliding
44 Platform
45 Jazz singer Jones
46 Kitchen kings
47 Flowering shrub
48 Great Pyramid builder
50 After six or square
51 Up to now
54 Art for public gardens
55 Belong
56 Mussel genus
58 Theosophist's degree
59 1929 Porter hit
60 Killing
62 Trombonist Conniff
65 Adage, briefly
66 James Gould's early editions?
69 Bulwer-Lytton heroine
70 Draw together
71 Managing editor's concern
72 Large pitcher
73 Change turf
74 World chess champ: 1894–1921

DOWN

1 Smidgens
2 Of aircraft
3 Russel's lookout?
4 Escaped
5 Six-time homer champ
6 ___-do-well
7 Early calculator
8 W.C. Handy's music
9 Candy for John?
10 Millstone
11 Envelope abbrs.
12 Pedantic like Jane?
13 "Elegy on Mrs. Mary ___": Goldsmith
14 Square-dance figure
15 Looks of contempt
20 Passover meal
24 Sun. missives
26 John with writer's block?
27 Majorcan port
29 Singlefoot, for one
30 Nasser's successor
31 Parisian possessive
33 Millennia
34 "The Poisoned Stream" author
35 Regal Norse names
37 Edgar's anthologies?
39 Bret's sob story?
40 Writer James and family
41 Grizzly
43 Worn-out
44 Some are hot
46 Area of a bird's bill
47 Asian sheep
49 Roll response
50 Impassive
51 Flower child
52 Lined up
53 Elite seat
54 Refined flour
57 Homesickness: Comb. form
60 Monkey puzzle
61 Highway tax
63 Seraph of Sèvres
64 River to the North Sea
66 When it flies, it's "fight" time
67 Pakistan president: 1978–88
68 Sphalerite, to chemists

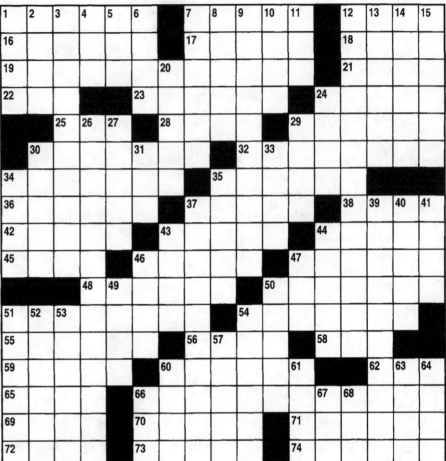

19 ACCORDING TO ... by Gayle Dean
Some whist-ful words from a legendary gamesman.

ACROSS

1. Medieval buffoon
7. Hyde Park transport
11. Biblical spy
16. Novelist Feuillet
17. Green feature
18. Lithe
19. **Start of Rule 12**
21. River past Amiens
22. Mauna ___
23. Reckoning
24. Close, e.g.
26. Table protector
28. Wharf
30. Interpret
31. Greet
33. Auburn's conference
34. Ripening agent
36. Bump off: Slang
39. Grommet
41. Cavalry sword
43. Maple genus
44. Copies
46. Prohibit
47. Bank deposit?
48. **End of Rule 12**
51. Envy
54. Feedbag bit
55. Angered
59. Bowled over
60. Drizzly
62. Crescent-shaped
63. Dramatist Jonson
64. "Der Corregidor" composer
65. Poet Lowell
67. Grouch
68. Catchall abbr.
70. "Jenny" star
72. Ryan or Greenfield
73. Vasco da Gama's ship
76. Sleep disturbance
78. Buffoon
81. Make joyful
82. **Author of Rule 12**
85. Not now
86. Energizer of sorts
87. City on the Trinity River
88. Wedding cake features
89. Ripped
90. Birch-family members

DOWN

1. Uppercut landing zone
2. Lover of Narcissus
3. Hotter
4. Thrash
5. Give the boot
6. Truckee River city
7. Sound teaching method?
8. Interstate
9. Father's robe
10. Colombian river
11. Roller
12. Greek marketplace
13. Edward Lear poem
14. Samara sources
15. Apiary residents
20. Fall guy
25. "After All" singer
27. Permitted
29. Capital of Morocco
31. Curse
32. Skipper's okay
33. Violist Broman
35. Sort
37. Terrific finish?
38. Drop a stitch
40. Way out
42. Helps
43. Obliquely
45. Tuffet
47. Stocking shade
49. City at the foot of Mt. Carmel
50. With thorough understanding
51. Taxi
52. Be outstanding?
53. Idolize
56. Grotesque waterspout
57. H-shaped letter
58. Society teen
60. Beauty spot
61. Pollywog
64. Falters
66. American educator Horace
69. Spud
71. More feeble
72. Taj ___
73. Prehistoric tool
74. Western branch of the Tien Shan
75. Liberal
77. Icelandic prose
79. Winged
80. Admit to (with "up")
83. Twosome
84. Wharton's "___ New York"

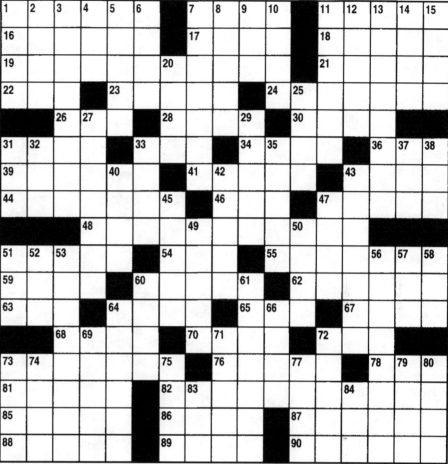

20 ANIMALIA   by Jill Winslow
How fitting the song title at 43 Across!

ACROSS

1 Slump
4 Tell all
8 Home of the Minoan civilization
13 Equal
17 Abbr. at Logan
18 Kansas town
19 "The Taming of the Shrew" setting
20 King in I Kings
21 Wahine's wreath
22 McNeile's adventurer
25 Singer Stuarti
27 Fourth dimension
28 Ending for Caesar
29 Chose
30 Drinking bowls
32 Med. suffixes
34 Chalon-___-Saône
36 Class for US immigrants
37 Equivocate
38 Dry
39 Middling
40 Jeanne, e.g.
41 Australian witch doctor
43 "Wild World" singer
46 Mound stat
47 Give a hand to
49 Allege
50 Fratricide victim
54 Tack on
55 Ill. neighbor
56 Sympathetic one
58 Unimpressed
59 Joshed
61 Sci-fi writer Card
62 Comely
63 Eastern monks
64 Not fitting
65 "Loose Connections" star
66 Newman's magazine
67 Adamson's animal
68 Fresh
69 Weakly
70 Wore away
71 Doodyville resident
75 Big Bertha's birthplace
77 Wheel
80 Brioche
81 Show
82 Turncoat
83 Old French shield
84 Orinoco tributary
85 "___ She Sweet?"
86 Ancient ascetic
89 Grow tardy
91 Kiddy card game
93 Greenish blue
95 Libido
96 Sue Charlton's love
100 Pose for a portrait
101 Litter member
102 Growing outward
103 Break bread
104 Carbohydrate suffix
105 ___ buco (veal dish)
106 Snowy bird
107 Male caribou
108 No, in Cape Town

DOWN

1 Town near Roanoke
2 Dean Smith Center, e.g.
3 TV woodsman
4 Overall part
5 Boors
6 "___ Want for Christmas" (1991)
7 Scottish cap
8 Naval noncom
9 Fads
10 Sturluson's prose
11 Relinquishes
12 ___ Claire, WI
13 "___ and Circumstance"
14 Behaves theatrically
15 Composer Chausson
16 Enigma

23 Resign
24 Idiot
26 ___ de-boeuf
31 Prepares
33 Promos
35 Addict
38 Sch.
39 Heptad
41 Fab Four member
42 Trying experience
44 Soothsayer's card
45 Garage event
48 Finale
51 He captured Dave Rudabaugh
52 Manor
53 W Netherlands city
56 Swimming stroke
57 Uraeus figure
58 Donkeys, e.g.
60 Swedish car
61 "Faithful" star
62 Sty
64 Static

65 Cartoonist Goldberg
68 ___ effort
69 Foreshadows
72 Heavens: Comb. form
73 Sapporo sash
74 African language
76 RSVP enclosure
77 Shoelace alternative
78 Wax-winged flier
79 Affectations
85 Rugged ridge
86 Verdugo in "The Boss's Son"
87 Din
88 Perfumer Lauder
90 Ghostbusters' car
92 Having wings
94 Miner's way in
97 Ruby in "Jungle Fever"
98 Let it be given: Rx
99 Brain test

21 WATER WORLD STARS   by Norman S. Wizer
Don't look for Kevin Costner below!

ACROSS

1 Damages
5 A tbs. consists of three
9 Ann or May
13 It comes out of the blue
17 Olive genus
18 Have a go ___
19 Turkish generals
20 "The ___ love . . ."
21 Talk-show host
23 Kind of jockey
24 Harrison or Coward
25 By reputation
26 "Designing Women" star
28 Drive
29 Fancy spread
30 ___ de deux
31 "Heat Wave" singer
35 "And I Love ___": Beatles
36 La followers
39 Crazy birds
40 Undecided
41 Lower level
43 Blunder
44 Hera's hubby
45 Suffix for Michael
46 Strange
47 Court at Wimbledon
50 "Stand by Me" star
54 Maltreat
56 Sam Spade's lawyer
57 Calendar abbr.
58 Dixieland trumpeter
63 Guevara's commander
67 Biblical land
68 Poseidon's call
69 "The ___ of Amontillado": Poe
71 Creek
72 Slandered
75 Gender abbr.
76 Hit it off
78 French pronoun
79 Closure
80 "In Lonesome Dove" singer
82 "Alice" spinoff
83 Muscle fitness
84 Filled cookie

85 "Suddenly" singer
89 Slouches
93 Circle
94 Western buddy
95 "Upstairs, Downstairs" actress
97 Special agent
98 Gaelic
99 Move quickly
100 Active place
101 Cartoonist Ketcham
102 It can be good or dirty
103 Artifice
104 Weakens

DOWN

1 Bad jokes
2 Mishmash
3 Clique
4 Recess
5 Soap ingredient
6 "Come early, ___"
7 Water ___ (teeth cleaner)
8 Fr. martyr
9 Military school roll
10 Perky
11 Kind of tense
12 Breaks out
13 Certain game show round
14 ___ about (around)
15 Garlic cousin
16 Mah-jongg piece
22 Stars, to fans
26 Shucks!
27 Mere
29 Is dogged
31 Pwr. source
32 Raced
33 Cornucopia
34 Turn at duty
35 Fasteners
36 Adolescent
37 Letters on a cross
38 Charon's river
41 Code or chart type

42 Sporting events
44 Zippo
45 Social Security program
48 Recurrent pattern
49 Vallone in "Bitter Rice"
51 Rome street
52 Dickens
53 WW2 agcy.
55 Mulled over
58 Green veggies
59 Other
60 Bugle call
61 Make a sign
62 Boss Tweed's nemesis
64 Bee Gees, e.g.
65 "Casablanca" hero
66 Twelve ___ (Tara's neighbor)
70 Savants
73 Trust

74 Pried
75 "Death in Venice" author
76 Kind of pie
77 Sponges
80 Egged on
81 "The Old Stoic" poet
82 Side
83 Succinct
85 Avon spa
86 "My Friend ___" (1949)
87 "Blithe Spirit" director
88 Have feelings for
90 Assam silkworm
91 Invitation letters
92 "___ My Gal"
95 Oil magnate's monogram
96 ___ de Cologne

22 FOOD FOR THOUGHT   by Brad Wilber
Dieters may wish to put this one on the back burner.

ACROSS

1 Ravi Shankar's instrument
6 Elated
12 Wild cards, at times
18 Desert brick
19 Dolls up
20 Dry ravine
21 "A nice hearty lunch . . ."
23 Capsule alternative
24 Like some prices
25 Director McCarey
26 Smelter's material
27 Start of MGM's motto
28 Shell game, e.g.
31 Sensationalized
33 Chignon site
36 Chromatic nuances
38 Cargo weight
39 Elkins of whodunits
40 Excessively glib
43 "Osso buco for dinner . . ."
46 Mil. decoration
47 Shapeless mass
49 Fin-de-siècle feeling
50 Elvis chart-topper of 1958
51 Salon dollop
52 Typographical ornament
54 Wedding cake section
55 Electrician, often
57 Rose
59 Former Pirate catcher
62 Watergate Trial evidence
64 Long Island airport town
66 English housecleaner
68 "Brigadoon" scorer
70 Unit of animation
72 Cash, slangily
74 Harvest goddess
76 Lose it
77 Minerva's symbol
78 "And of course, dessert!"
80 Do wedelns
81 Substantive
83 Old French coin
84 Yothers and Majorino
86 Mischievous
87 Stews
89 Delicacy
90 Half of the NFL
93 Promotional blitzes
95 Hellenic vowel
97 Contralto Dominguez
99 Liszt Museum site
101 "I'd like some fruit, I think . . ."
104 Call into question
105 Kin of a virginal
106 "A Lonely Rage" author
107 Tousles
108 Picked up on
109 Down-at-heel

DOWN

1 Pelvic bones
2 Faineant
3 Tipsters
4 "S.O.S." singers
5 Oppose
6 Economist Tinbergen
7 Idiosyncratic
8 Caterwaul
9 Bay window
10 Crass
11 Librarian's admonition
12 Saw socially
13 Part of QED
14 Champaign's neighbor
15 "Can't forget the veggies . . ."
16 Peacock plume feature
17 Dipso
22 Place for a bookcase
26 Gilligan's boat
29 Concerning
30 Scrooge
32 ___ atlas
34 Accommodate Avedon
35 Organic compound
37 Fishtailed
39 Type of projection
40 "Masterpiece Theatre" network
41 Rathskeller orders
42 "A crunchy snack sounds good . . ."
44 Bogart film
45 Emulate Mme. Defarge
48 Lives
53 Like Garrison Keillor stories
56 "Beowulf," for one
58 Use a rotary phone
60 It can be grand
61 La Brea attraction
63 Envelope inits.
65 Cutting tool
67 Queen, in Spain
69 Finial
70 Robin Cook bestseller
71 Washstand item
73 Behold, to Brutus
75 Manatee
79 Erato's sister
82 An endocrine gland
85 Reiterate
87 Adder's-tongues
88 Besmirch
90 Pool menace
91 "Places in the Heart" star
92 Record spinner Kasem
94 Beep
96 Reinking and Sothern
98 "Zip-___-Doo-Dah"
99 Director Wenders
100 Ostrich relative
101 CIA forerunner
102 Turn right
103 LAX abbr.

23 DEMEANINGS   by Bert Rosenfield
Have you ever heard of a laxicographer? (Bert is one.)

ACROSS

1 Legal thing
4 Pay up
9 Palm off
12 Timberlane of fiction
16 Clarifies
19 Southern constellation
20 Muscat's country
21 Best place for de wash?
22 Bread for Li'l Abner
24 ___-Dame de Paris
25 Rambling
27 Stature
28 Hydroxyl compounds
29 Prefix with sol or stat
30 Textile machine device
31 Tent furnishings
32 Bilk an entire island?
36 Cádiz crafts
37 Borneo macaque
38 Cartoonist Young
39 Nearing bedtime
41 Windward island
42 He left Troy in flames
45 "Sons and Lovers" actress
46 God or asteroid
50 Snee's relative
51 Made one's flesh crawl
53 Ambience
54 Protest of the '60s
57 Aviator Balbo
58 To the point
59 Paeans
60 Fire Bonzo?
62 Termagants
64 Bogus deity
65 Doggie-bag morsel
66 Loser at Chalons in 451
68 Amalgamation: Abbr.
71 Dreamy combiner
74 Addict
75 James Bond's superior
76 Gran ___, S.A.
79 K-9 weapon?
82 Troy oz. subdivs.
83 Tie in
85 Colima curl
86 Preakness winner: 1942
87 Vinegary
88 Billy Wilder film
90 Sicily's neighbor
91 Shaped like a prow
93 Male land?
95 Cartoonist Soglow
96 "___ Rheingold"
97 Walked a hazardous line
98 Free gradually
99 Saucehound
100 Break off
101 Object of an SDS protest

DOWN

1 Rowdies
2 Italian tragedienne Duse
3 Underwater craft inventory?
4 "The Sun Also ___"
5 Nigerian city near Ibadan
6 Long-running musical
7 Repetition
8 Madagascar insectivore
9 Statistic
10 Granada gold
11 Fonteyn's rail
12 Police chiefs?
13 Entirety
14 South Carolina river
15 Dirty looks
17 Sagan and Sandburg
18 Bart or Belle
23 Yellowish-greens
26 Christmas carol
32 "Bang Bang" singer
33 Comment from the sty
34 Bullish prefix
35 ___ gris (befuddled)
38 No. 2 man
40 Past-participle ending
43 Nora's canine
44 ___ Flow, Orkney Islands
47 Capek classic
48 Siderite, for one
49 Neill or Nunn
50 Where Durante was at?
52 Play ___ (serve over)
54 Blubber
55 Rhoda's mom
56 Cha or Bohea
57 Dorsey lead-in
58 Gelling agent
60 Cedar Rapids college
61 Jejune
62 Decree ___ (divorce prelim)
63 Pianist Templeton
67 Office of a mentor
68 Bovine undergarments?
69 Boiled-dinner ingredients
70 Breaks up
72 Absent
73 Grimm figure
76 Polish city on the Vistula
77 Goddess of witchcraft
78 "Watch out, Miguel!"
80 Hub
81 Containing nitrates
82 Aristotle's teacher
84 Modified organisms
86 To love, in Livorno
88 Song or slug follower
89 ___ Mohammed Khan
92 Confucian truth
94 PMs

ACROSS

1 Rolle or Williams
7 Sedated
12 Former Philippine president
18 Psychotic one, for short
19 Mountain ridge
20 Come forth
21 Material dessert?
23 Dead Sea fortress
24 Shred
25 Austrian city
26 Bedouins and Berbers
28 Poivre's partner
29 Orchestra member
31 Zero-trick bid
34 Before, to bards
35 "Die Frau ___ Schatten": Strauss
36 Emulates Niobe
38 Keeps a date
40 Refuse
42 Baton
44 "Three Blind ___ "
46 Slain Canaanite commander
49 Material creatures?
53 Locale of 37 Down
54 Immediately!
57 Burdened
58 "Wind in the Willows" hero
60 Give forth
61 Writer Santha Rama ___
62 "Clan of the Cave Bear" author
63 "How Sweet ___!"(1968)
65 Butyl ending
66 Tennessee's flower
68 Garage event
70 "Wake of the Ferry" painter
71 Hardin and Cobb
72 Zip
74 Material sport?
77 Menu listing
79 Change the decor
80 Hannibal Smith's group
83 John Wayne was one
85 Bellamy or Bunche
88 Black buck of India
90 Laborer
92 Johnny of the CSA
94 John Paul II, born ___ Wojtyla
96 Husband, in Hyeres
97 Finnish actress Taina
98 Tool for Figaro
100 Vicinity
102 Varnish resin
103 Church protocol
105 Material timer?
109 Whale's leap
110 Whodunit hints
111 Ripken, for one
112 "We're off to ___ wizard . . ."
113 Be noncommittal
114 Carrot's cousin

DOWN

1 Money held in trust
2 Early journalists
3 O'Neill's "A Touch of ___ "
4 Au courant, slangily
5 Dusseldorf donkey
6 Violinist's need
7 Wow
8 Galena or bauxite
9 Fondle
10 Comical Kett
11 Maximizer Combine maker
12 Club roster
13 "Amo, ___, I love a lass": O' Keeffe
14 Legal matter
15 Material headgear?
16 Poet Nash
17 Douglas in "Aladdin"
22 E pluribus ___
27 Part of MoMA
30 "The Iliad," e.g.
32 Slot-machine fruit
33 Of the ear
35 Davis in "The Client"
37 La ___ (opera house)
39 Shoo!
41 Goal
43 Actor Brandauer
45 Prima ballerina
47 "___ Night in Georgia"
48 Poker pennies
50 Paradigm
51 Crawlspace cousin
52 Squelched
54 After booby or door
55 "Mack the Knife" crooner
56 Material insect?
59 Paul Anka hit
64 Fits of temper
67 Young haddock
69 Washstand pitcher
70 Poppaea Sabina's robe
73 Chop down
75 Neighbor of Minn.
76 Sewing line
78 Dumbo's dreaded affliction?
81 Crazy ___
82 Wonderwork
84 Pince-___
86 Laud
87 Giraffe feature
89 ___-and-dime (small-time)
90 Parsley, sage, rosemary, and thyme
91 Cloister walk
93 Make a hash of
95 ___ lamb
98 Like Bill Gates
99 Rub the wrong way
101 Farm unit
104 Grandma's hair pad
106 Cow's chew
107 Beer container
108 "Flight of the Innocents" author

MINCED WORDS   by Cathy Millhauser
Cathy has a talent for finding unique themes, like this one.

ACROSS

1 Joab's victim
8 S.A. grassy plain
13 Painter Durand
18 "Pinocchio" author
19 Town N of Yakutsk
20 Bit of drudgery
21 NAGASAKI
23 Recreate
24 Back in time
25 Esteemed congregation member
26 Rumpelstiltskin's spinning
27 CASTANET
32 "Wabbit" hunter
35 Kajar Dynasty's domain
38 Carol on covers
39 Hoopster Archibald
41 "National Velvet" horse
42 Louis XIV's coin
43 Confederate
45 Lake of Geneva resort
46 Dominoes one
47 Tritons' trumpets
49 TAGALOG
52 Medleys
53 They're striking
55 Venus, e.g.
56 ___ Fein
57 Epps and Sharif
58 Jaunt
61 "___ the season . . ."
63 Ruffled
65 He caught Larsen's perfect game
66 PANAMA
69 Like some auricles
71 "Fantasy Island" mermaid
72 Joyce and Raines
73 Polynesian idol
74 "Les Nuits d'___": Berlioz
75 Even one
76 British clink
77 Br. military award
79 Deeply instilled
81 Pooch from China
83 BUCKAROO
86 Mechanical mutt in "Sleeper"
88 Offers orisons
89 Cosell's field, once
92 Stemmed
94 FUNDA-MENTAL-IST
99 "Algiers" star
100 Forearm bones
101 Parsons in "Bonnie and Clyde"
102 Sneak laterally
103 "Night Music" dramatist
104 Fingers

DOWN

1 Surgeons' org.
2 ___ Raton
3 Trudge
4 Apportions
5 City near Jerusalem
6 Psychic in "Ghost"
7 "Giant" actor
8 Near the tail
9 Bear witness
10 Slalom medalist Phil
11 Quid–quo link
12 Dinghy adjunct
13 Height: Comb. form
14 Mantelpiece, for one
15 PROPAGATE
16 Time piece?
17 Sgt. Preston's horse
22 Poetic "forever"
26 Reach
28 Weather-map markings
29 Almost extinct
30 Contrary
31 Hand weapons?
33 They're thrown in Monopoly
34 Pronghorn
35 Rio Grande feeder
36 Rod-shaped bacteria
37 RAMADAN
40 "Geraint and ___": Tennyson
44 Balaam's mount
45 Big Band singer Ray
48 Like a dunce cap
49 Bounds
50 In the least
51 Doled
54 Fools, a la Puck
59 In high dudgeon
60 Walked nervously
62 Keel part
63 One with convictions?
64 Year in St. Gregory's papacy
65 Sell for
66 Hillock
67 Niblick's number
68 Actor Brandauer
70 Related
73 1964 Olympic site
77 "Doggone!"
78 Equilibrium
80 Fonteyn's forte
82 Toulouse-Lautrec's tripod
84 Horatian poetry form
85 Comparable to a beet
87 "Primal Fear" star
90 Confederate
91 Stairway shaft
92 Workout target
93 Hugh Capet, e.g.
94 Socko sign
95 Digs
96 Juliette Low's org.
97 Lister's last word
98 Legal matter

26 LINE FOR THE FRONTLINE   by Alfio Micci

This truth from twenty-six centuries ago is still relevant.

ACROSS

1 Greek square
6 Huxtable and Rehan
10 Overtook
16 Blackouts
17 As ___ (generally)
18 "La Strada" director
19 Former Barbary state
20 Discharge
21 1996 Olympic site
22 **Start of a moral**
25 Matriculates
26 Hun king
27 Bionomics: Abbr.
30 ___ Kippur
33 Cassette insert
34 Actor's help
35 Honshu city
36 Nail paints
38 Like a roué
41 ___-a-porter
42 Icy
43 Chums
44 Run in
46 Crossword diagram
47 Stalin's secret-police chief
49 Goes on a spree
51 **The story (with "The")**
54 Devotion
57 "People Are Strange" group
58 Verve
62 Shows its face
63 Japanese aborigine
64 Hibernation sound
65 Weaverbird's weaving
66 Climb
69 Give orders
71 "Swinging ___ Star"
72 Cannes chum
73 "I ___ man with seven . . ."
74 Nourished
75 Hildegarde in "Svengali"
77 Don King's rival
78 Jet star, e.g.
80 **End of a moral**
86 Botanical interstices
88 Shades
89 "___ every little star . . ."
90 Alarms
91 Jagged
92 Where Hercules fought a lion
93 System
94 Fender flaw
95 Currycomb

DOWN

1 Play start
2 Toe ailment
3 Arena at 21 Across
4 Up
5 Gave a nod
6 Kind of plaid
7 Music for two
8 "The Sun ___ Rises"
9 Reversals
10 Lab dish
11 Actress Nazimova
12 Bondsman
13 Soft jobs
14 Tolkien creature
15 Day, in Spain
17 Source of 51 Across (with 18 Down)
18 See 17 Down
23 Inland sea
24 Needle case
28 Stout
29 Riga natives
30 Safecracker
31 Lulu
32 Bamako is its capital
37 Central America?
38 Weather forecast
39 Disney film
40 Lends an ear
41 Wise
43 Beseech
45 Newspaperman Ottley
47 Happiness
48 Salamander
49 Debussy's daughter
50 ___ Lingus
52 Miss or Bull
53 Fashionable
54 Orale
55 A Worth
56 Alienate
59 Bread unit
60 Funny Johnson
61 Exigency
63 Lively
64 Fitzgerald's forte
67 Bother
68 Don of talk radio
69 Passing
70 "Play ___ It Lays": Didion
73 Unassuming
76 Beanie wearer
77 Correct
78 Fitted piece
79 "Cimarron" is one
81 Hodgepodge
82 Links cry
83 "It Ain't Gonna Rain ___"
84 Liz role
85 Cheese in a ball
86 CIRRUS machine
87 Caviar

"GOOD EVENING!"   by Nancy Scandrett Ross
Some mysterious wordplay involving 69 Across.

ACROSS

1 Bath and Baden
5 Neil Diamond hit
9 Yawn
13 New wine
17 Court score
18 Ye ___ tea shoppe
19 Notion
20 Extremely draftworthy
21 Cartoonist Graham
22 Ma Bell's favorite film?
25 Dizzy Gillespie's favorite film?
27 Permit
28 They sleep outdoors
29 Stretches (with "out")
30 Bottom line
32 Magi guide
33 One in a box
36 Cheryl of opera
39 Pluto's Roman counterpart
42 Sound of disgust
43 River through Bern
44 Cleaning cloth
46 Ticket-order encl.
47 David Copperfield's favorite film?
54 "Treasure Island" beggar
55 Foolish
56 Catullus lyric
57 Tarot suit
59 Turkish official
60 Latin conjugation starter
61 M. Hulot portrayer
62 Goddess of ghosts
64 In the manner of
65 Faultfinders
68 Showery mo.
69 Master of suspense
73 Prevarications
75 Sycophant's word
76 Ending for Manhattan
77 Kanga's child
78 Group of eight
80 Contribute
83 Faces
86 Sale words
88 Negative adverb
89 Stagehand
90 Kabul native
93 Colorado Indian
95 De Mornay's favorite film?
99 Hedonist's favorite film? (with "The")
102 Valueless
103 Counting-out word
104 Roosevelt terrier
105 "L'Africaine" soprano
106 Periods
107 Pre-college exams
108 Sensed
109 Grant in "North By Northwest"
110 Test-drive car

DOWN

1 Bulgar or Croat
2 May Day sight
3 Declare positively
4 Half-dozen
5 Drysdale was one
6 Hodgepodges
7 G&S princess
8 Rossini hero
9 Exceptionally talented
10 Fuss
11 Saucy
12 Turn-of-the-century Met diva
13 Masonry materials
14 Giles Goat-Boy's favorite film?
15 Oracle
16 "H.M.S. Pinafore" chorus members
23 Carte du jour
24 Golden Rule word
26 Well-liked president
31 Succinct
33 Common conjunction
34 Muslim title
35 Mole's favorite film?
36 Conserve
37 Refrain syllable
38 Cheer word
40 Played for a sucker
41 Bastes
43 Rand of letters
45 Of dance movements
48 Capital in the Andes
49 "West Side Story" girl
50 Dreadfully
51 Itinerant
52 "What'll ___?": Berlin
53 Cut a ___ (create a stir)
58 Auricular
60 Grogshop fare
62 Angelic circle
63 Vergilian
64 Firebug's crime
65 Quote
66 Map abbr.
67 Tom Conti, for one
70 Nourished
71 Thwack
72 Joe Louis had 21
74 Moves nonchalantly
79 Buenos ___
81 Chewy candy
82 Ant genus
83 Crazy Eddie's favorite film?
84 Tease
85 Began a theatrical season
87 Tobacco product
89 Garson of Hollywood
90 Gibbons
91 Pet pest
92 Dies ___
94 Ambler or Clapton
96 Nostrum
97 Quahog
98 Too
100 Pipe elbow
101 Genetic monogram

28 THE NAME GAME by Fred Piscop
As played by our Long Island punster.

ACROSS

1 "There's ___ of hush . . ."
6 Sidi ___, Morocco
10 Moisten the plants
14 Exaggerator's suffix
17 Crusoe creator
18 The Kennedys, e.g.
19 "B.C." predator
21 Coach Berry?
23 Con Charles?
24 Feel crummy
25 French seaport
27 "Grumpier Old Men" star
28 "___ Are": Mathis
32 Art Deco designer
33 "Able was I ___ . . ."
34 Ullmann in "Lost Horizon"
35 Slangy so-long
37 Bullpen stats
39 Give off
43 Western tribe
44 Aer Lingus flight attendant?
47 Hersey hamlet
48 Author Ephron
50 Tapir feature
51 Laura in "A Perfect World"
53 Monopoly quartet: Abbr.
54 Pol's payoff
56 Sign up
58 Bestows
60 "After Hours" star
62 St. ___ Fire
64 Spanish surrealist
65 Samuel Francis Smith composition
68 Enjoy to the max
70 Most piddling
73 Scott's "The ___ Quartet"
74 Christmastime trio
76 Fork features
78 Erato's sister
79 Coagulates
81 Barbash of AFL-CIO fame?
84 Advisor Landers
85 Toast topper
86 Lions and tigers
87 Post-workout woe
88 Act the stoolie
89 ___ di-dah
91 Greek vowels
94 Hubert ___ Humphrey
96 Vibrant
98 Bruce Willis film
100 Minn. neighbor
101 Motorist McMahon?
103 Make Cosby twice as great?
108 Iron ore
109 Humorist Bombeck
110 Lash of westerns
111 AMA members
112 Feeder filler
113 Famed loch
114 He invented the huddle

DOWN

1 Recipe word
2 Plunk preceder
3 "___ Fell": Beatles
4 Strikeout king Ryan
5 Corpus ___
6 I, as in Innsbruck
7 Screw up
8 Mother-of-pearl
9 Signatory
10 Produced a studio tape
11 S&L earnings
12 Subway entrances
13 Kind of sax
14 Raison d'___
15 Writer O'Faolain
16 Put to the test
20 "It's a deal!"
22 Takes home
26 Cancel a cancellation
28 Emulated a limpet
29 ___-miss
30 Calculate what DiMaggio batted?
31 "Goosebumps" books author
36 In unison
38 Overwhelmed
40 Bellicose Buchwald?
41 Concerning
42 Deep-six
45 Takes the mound
46 Mouth: Comb. form
47 Historical record
49 Way off
52 Curtain fixture
55 Tonsorial touch-ups
57 The ___ Spoonful
59 Clunes in "Richard III"
61 ___ Victor
63 Ice queen Henie
65 Sacramento arena
66 Shopper's heaven
67 Rio Grande filler
69 Get in touch with
71 Egyptian peninsula
72 Spanish fool
75 Spouse-to-be
77 Sheridan's "The ___ for Scandal"
80 "One Life ___"
82 Proportion words
83 Gists
86 "My ___ Amour": 1969 tune
90 Declares
92 "Our Miss Brooks" star
93 Emporium
95 Up, in Camden Yards
96 Bone-dry
97 Toppers
99 Eschews the lyrics
101 British medal
102 Nancy's summer
104 ___-relief
105 A Gershwin
106 Schlep
107 ___-pull (hoax)

29 ACTOR'S ACTOR by Fran and Lou Sabin
He's been in thousands of crosswords. This is all him!

ACROSS

1 French radical: 1743–93
6 More intrusive
12 Calced
17 "Heaven Can Wait" star (1943)
19 Part of POG
20 Berry in "Boomerang"
21 1965 film featuring 51 Down
23 Surface
24 Write "supercede"
25 Strange position?
26 Out of sight
27 Shrewd
28 Debtor's note
29 Valued highly
31 After third
32 Dig site
34 Locane of "Melrose Place"
35 Firing-line line
36 Christmassy color
39 Memo starter
40 Piedmont province
42 Boston cager, for short
44 Film featuring 51 Down (with 88 Down)
45 Frank's place?
47 "Darn it!"
48 Hunt for water
49 Celestial altar
52 Jane Tennison, e.g.
55 Pointer sister
56 Pagodaroof
58 Artist Veronese
59 Mug
60 Covent Garden fare
61 Film, 1967, featuring 51 Down ("The")
63 Give a hard time
64 Ringlets
65 Carducci's "Primitive ___"
66 Tykes
68 Schleps
69 Double-crosser
70 Publisher Conde
72 Salary factors
76 Alphabet run
77 Cartoonist Key
78 Swabbie
79 Capri or May
80 Okoboji is here
82 Choppy
87 Assam or keemun
88 "Shadow-lands" star
90 It's eaten in pieces
91 Slangy turndown
92 Hammer's forte
93 Designer Simpson
94 1966 film featuring 51 Down
97 Gadget button
98 Iris portion
99 Wall Street employee
100 Brattish
101 Klemperer in "Hogan's Heroes"
102 Noted film critic

DOWN

1 Dessert wine
2 Like honeymooners
3 Sign up
4 Make a move
5 Gunwale pin
6 Kobe amusement
7 Kobe craft
8 Lip-smacking good
9 Simpleminded
10 Provoked
11 Classic car
12 Haifa greeting
13 Male seal's devotees
14 1948 film featuring 51 Down
15 Other
16 Pronghorn
18 Gray in "Silver Spoons"
22 Majors' last letter
27 Receipt
30 Wear away
33 Silent acceptance
35 Spiny-leafed plant
37 Island of giant statues
38 Feeling listless
40 "Shake ___!"
41 Brood
42 Nanny's ward
43 Poem's last stanza
44 Certain juniors
46 Best and O'Brien
47 Siouans
48 1989 Tandy role
49 Bikini et al.
50 Remove roughly
51 Legendary British actor
53 Verse form
54 Spin on ice
57 Nettles
59 Anchor bend
61 "Betty ___": 1930 hit
62 Iron pumper's pride
67 Bill Nye's subj.
69 Take testimony from
70 Airplane engine enclosure
71 Pigskin path
73 In the saddle
74 Crowd chaser
75 Perth or Brisbane
77 Sylvester's obsession
78 Load
81 Goatish glances
82 Ozawa reading material
83 Mickey
84 Santa from Mexico
85 Biting
86 Windy City hub
88 See 44 Across
89 Conceit
94 Dobbin's "left!"
95 Equality
96 Wee bit

30 TURNING GREEN   by Cathy Millhauser
The theme for this puzzle has a truly remarkable twist.

ACROSS

1 Groupie group
5 Gingrich
9 Tours "with"
13 Glengarry kin
16 Tracy Marrow's rap name
17 Berg
18 Maui neighbor
20 "Warszawa" instrumentalist
21 Green disaster area?
24 "Them!" giant
25 Cut off
26 Tse-tung supporter
27 Kind of paper
29 Ohio college
32 Carole King song re green?
34 King Arthur's foster brother
35 Regard
36 Reveals
37 Book about a green veggie?
43 Rub ___ (aggravate)
45 "The Way We ___"
46 Basso Pinza
47 Goldwater, e.g.
51 Ring holders
52 Cry for Manolete
54 Pert song
55 Crossword coach
56 LeGallienne and Gabor
57 Back when one was green?
60 Printing directive
61 Satori-seeking sect
62 Masking, for one
63 AMA members
64 Mackerel cousin
65 Interlaces
67 "¿Como ___?"
70 Bahai homeland
71 Unique being
72 Green actress?
75 Truffaut's "passion"
78 Surrounded by
80 Lever part
81 Hymn to a green stone?
83 Stretch
87 Monitor flasher
88 "___ Pieces": Peter & Gordon hit
90 Shack
92 Former HEW/HHS division
93 Seeing-green sensation?
97 SASE, for one
98 Abbie Hoffman's group, e.g.
99 Memo starter
100 Gagne of baseball
101 Ferdinand the Great was one
102 An NCO
103 Tour de force
104 Rochester's beloved

DOWN

1 Suits
2 Pined
3 Chutzpah
4 "Grace Before Meat" painter
5 Patriots org.
6 An Ivy Leaguer
7 LPGA members
8 Magazine for minors
9 French province, formerly
10 Luggage piece
11 Alfonso's queen
12 Poetic chapter
13 Bristly plant
14 Marigold, e.g.
15 AAA listings
19 Make a fool of
22 Eleniak in "Chasers"
23 "As ___ and breathe!"
28 Translated notes?
30 Tempura aperitif
31 Courtroom cry
33 Spiral
37 Pluck, in a way
38 State of bliss
39 Wandering
40 Stack or Costner role
41 Electron tubes
42 Punt propeller
44 Music curves
47 Wimbledon winner: 1992
48 Quality
49 Punta ___, Chile
50 Swimming
53 Conclusion
57 Strike setting
58 "Edgar" and "Norma"
59 ___ Scott decision
60 Cooler
62 Hot places for cats?
66 "The Caine Mutiny" author and family
68 Bender
69 Pick target
72 Angler's act
73 Music hall
74 Brando's birthplace
75 Zodiac figure
76 N Ireland river
77 Rule by: Suffix
79 "The Executioner's Song" writer
82 Detaches
83 "Hec Ramsey" star
84 Matt Dillon's city
85 Dosage word
86 "Over my dead body!"
89 Nine-to-fiver's slogan
91 Winter Olympics event
94 Just-prior period
95 Christian brother
96 "Ebony" competitor

STARS COME OUT AT NIGHT   by Brad Wilber

Here's a good one to solve in the PM.

ACROSS

1 High points
6 100 centimos
12 Cured herring
18 Inclined
19 Wood sorrel
20 Esoteric
21 Basketball's "Pistol"
23 Detroit cager
24 When the French fry
25 Basket fiber
26 Myanmar neighbor
28 Be penitent
29 Baryshnikov, originally
31 Make lacy edges
32 Boardwalk board
34 "How to Frame a ___" (Knotts movie)
35 Belgian balladeer
37 Not bold
38 Floppy-disk forerunner
39 Animal trail
41 Pester relentlessly
42 Abounding
43 Hearing aid?
44 Irascible
45 Hack
48 Minister to
49 Rugby segment
50 Modem sound
51 Dos Passos opus
52 Flying piscivore
53 "The Karate Kid" star
55 Put the kibosh on
56 No one in particular
57 Confreres
58 Paul of "Melvin and Howard"
59 ". . . till death ___ part"
60 "My Man Godfrey" star
62 Orion twinkler
63 Loosens
64 Burn balm
65 Golden Horde member
66 Salome's septet
67 BBQ garb
69 Programming language
70 Cutlery point
71 Elapsed
72 Riddle
73 Clinton's instrument
74 One of Lady Bird's daughters
78 Suffix for shrew
79 Dots in the drink
80 Began a line?
82 Mortals
83 Spectrum examiner
85 "Broadway Boogie-Woogie" painter
89 Singer Dion
90 Tigrillo
91 Demean
92 Goodman and Greene
93 Mortise complements
94 Exclamation of dread

DOWN

1 Fencing lunge
2 It's south of the Cyclades
3 Sacred composition
4 Chemical ending
5 Precious beginning
6 Ingress
7 Glorify
8 Salt away
9 Clockmaker Terry
10 Quirk
11 City of NE Kentucky
12 Pillow padding
13 Blue flag
14 "Surfing" necessities?
15 "Melba" star
16 Plenty
17 Back out
22 Daisy relative
27 Tamandua snack
30 Investment-portfolio item
32 1993 World Series MVP
33 Wrinkled
34 Actress d'Orsay
36 Hundred Acre Wood resident
37 L.A. arena
38 Idee ___
39 Canned heat
40 "Big" director
41 "The truth ___"
42 Charged
43 Peculate
44 Blanch
45 Utter
46 Digressions
47 Ariadne's isle
49 Exempt
50 Microwave feature
54 Stately
57 Medium-blue shade
59 Archangel in II Esdras 4
61 Aspersion
62 "Streamers" playwright
63 Marsh
65 Dipso
66 Stock soap character
67 Each
68 Ecru, for one
69 Playfully noncommittal
70 Cards with swords
72 Glazier units
73 Maestro Rattle
75 Eskimo boat
76 Discontinue
77 "The Wreck of the Mary Deare" novelist
79 Hartford loc.
80 Normandy city
81 June 6, 1944
84 Repose
86 Sometimes it's shaved
87 Twilight, to Tennyson
88 McGriff's stat

32 MALE BONDING by Dean Niles
Where's George Lazenby?

ACROSS

1 Old soft drink
5 Paper features
8 Blubber
12 Equanimity
17 Oodles
18 Hairbrush or toothbrush, e.g.
20 AOL message
21 "The Living Daylights" star
23 Amazing magician
24 Sugar suffix
25 Cartoonist Hokinson
26 Source of the Amazon
28 Italian monk
29 Flintstones' era
32 Big galoots
34 Nicosia locale
36 Einstein's birthplace
38 "Long time ___!"
39 Lothario
40 Chicago suburb
43 Philatelist's collection
46 Hotelier
49 Straggle
51 Pinnacle
52 More cunning
53 Esoteric deck
55 Impediment
56 Atmosphere: Comb. form
59 "Diamonds Are Forever" star
62 ABC show
63 Purloin
65 Wishful thinking
66 "Star" couples
68 Majestic
70 Camera type
71 Peaked
75 Antarctic covering
77 Sprinkle
79 Rhine feeder
80 Assessed
82 Chang's twin
83 "New Jack City" star
85 Sword of ___
88 Shaky desserts
91 Ginseng relative
92 Boons
94 "___ is an island": Donne
95 Breed
98 Newsstand
100 "GoldenEye" star
103 Dread-inducing
104 Stout
105 Graham of football
106 Fat-filled
107 Beliefs
108 TCU class
109 Cecil Day-Lewis, e.g.

DOWN

1 West. alliance
2 Yale Bowl hosts
3 Folksy
4 "Quincy, M.E." actor
5 Sparta's rival
6 Holmes' creator
7 Disc jockey's choice
8 ___ canto (singing style)
9 "___ Troll": Heine
10 Amiss
11 Hubert's 1964 running mate
12 Rides out
13 Wolfgang's grandma
14 "Diamonds Are Forever" author
15 Libyan gulf
16 Walt Disney's middle name
19 Lethargy
22 "___ Swell": Rodgers & Hart
27 Physical love
30 Voyages for Picard
31 Large cervid
33 Bounds
34 Dernier ___
35 Hither's partner
37 Lombardy city
40 Asparagus stalks
41 Piths
42 Breadwinner's preoccupation
44 Baby buggy
45 Nintendo rival
47 Golfer Ernie
48 Regarded
50 "Egmont" playwright
53 Dick and Harry's companion
54 Shoe stretcher
56 Field: Comb. form
57 Part of G.E.
58 "For Your Eyes Only" star
60 ___ diem
61 Songstress Sumac
64 Portuguese territory
67 Overwhelmed with humor
69 Opener
71 Dispatch
72 Gains access
73 Charlemagne's dom.
74 "Roundabout" group
76 Kilauea's goddess
78 Luanda loc.
81 Oracle seat
83 Kicks off
84 Señora's boy
85 James Madison team
86 Bye-bye, Brigitte
87 They're licensed to kill
89 Loamy deposit
90 Honey-colored
93 Junction
96 Recent
97 Gordius tied one
99 Mind
101 Campers, e.g.
102 Bribe

33 HIDDEN HINT   by Shirley Soloway
Solve the two long theme words and you'll find it.

ACROSS

1 "___ well that . . ."
5 Tortilla dish
9 Function
13 ___ with (interfere)
17 Cross
18 Image
19 Genesis shepherd
20 Motown product
21 Golfer Brett
22 Racer Bonnett
23 Emcee for NBC
24 Barrymore in "Mad Love"
25 **Hint to solvers: Part I**
29 NE Minnesota city
30 Pince-___
31 Henna, e.g.
32 Juice the goose
35 Lack
37 Judge's attribute
42 "Changes" singer
43 ___-Tiki
44 Walk out
46 Nothing
47 Graven image
48 Purple bloom
50 Lepus
51 Raison d' ___
52 Parchment
54 Argue
56 Scatter
57 Throw kisses at
59 Frighten
60 Vreeland of fashion
62 Delicate
64 Addicted
67 Laura Wingfield's mother
70 Words from Caesar
71 Grass
72 Coed complex
74 Env. science
75 From ___ Z
76 Improvise
78 Sack
79 "The Silencers" hero
80 Deceiving
82 Activate
84 At sixes and sevens
85 Trifle
86 Margin
87 Apply a rider

88 **Hint to solvers: Part II**
98 Enterprise navigator
99 Check proofs
100 Close to one's heart
101 Idyllist
102 Lundy, e.g.
103 Pushed a button
104 Ranee dress
105 Chalk out
106 Satellite hook-up
107 "Postcards From the ___":(1990)
108 Koala's home
109 Forearm bone

DOWN

1 From
2 Company symbol
3 Wunderkind
4 They have cushy jobs?
5 Cheap
6 Shot one
7 Hairstyle
8 Computer linked
9 Anniversary dance
10 Toe the line
11 City near Mount Rose
12 Yukon region
13 Infuriate
14 Brit or German
15 Bouillabaisse
16 Seeded
26 Shebeen quaff
27 T-men
28 Australian salt lake
32 French forest
33 "Back In Black" group
34 Cal Ripken's position
35 Negative conjunction
36 Patient wife

37 "Animal House" house
38 On radio
39 On-ramps
40 Pater
41 Raft
43 Brick-baking oven
45 Frost-freed
49 Billy Ripken's spot
51 Made cards more costly
53 Kind of brother
55 ___ choy
56 Mixologist Malone
58 Uniform color
61 Metrical foot
62 Raiment
63 "Leave ___ Beaver"
65 Orientalist Lattimore
66 Nerd
68 He ran with Ford

69 ___ mater
71 C'est ___
73 Lobster eggs
76 Queue before Q
77 Was in arrears
81 Flowed
83 Surrounded by
84 Dict. abbr.
86 Waffle
87 Condor's nest
88 Look___ (appear)
89 Artifice
90 Women's magazine
91 Best part
92 "Western Union" director
93 Approaching
94 Singular
95 "Rock 'n' ___ Mom" (1988)
96 Bean in "GoldenEye"
97 Mount in Sicily

STRIKE UP THE BAND   by A.J. Santora
A sense of humor is instrumental to solving this one.

ACROSS

1 "Elephant Boy" boy
5 Desertlike
9 Rowlands of films
13 Beer head
17 Mangle
18 "Boxiana" author
19 "The Talmadge Girls" author
20 "___ Room": Beach Boys
21 A harpist is always . . .
24 Stadium row
25 Bar seats
26 Sped off
27 "High Hopes" singer
29 Cherrystone
31 Coral deposit
33 Call for help
34 A guitarist . . .
38 Contest participants
43 Merkel in "The Kentuckian"
44 WW2 arena
45 Supermodel Macpherson
47 Wrong
48 Burl Ives, e.g.
52 Vibrancy
54 Swenson of "Benson"
55 Pokey
56 Bridge objectives
58 Most sunburned
60 Internet area
62 Arguments
64 Tied the knot
65 Gave in
69 Chick sounds
71 Envelope feature
74 "Big Raven" painter
75 Challenge
77 Caroused
80 Tumults
82 Shape
84 Canadian prov.
85 SEP sister
86 Delights
88 A pianist is always . . .
92 Special decade
93 "East of Eden" girl
95 Health retreats
96 John Goodman film
100 Bone prefix
102 Curved entryways
106 Southern-most US city
107 A trumpeter will always . . .
110 Woody's son
111 Waterford locale
112 Thompson of "Family"
113 Hollywood's Kazan
114 Uniformed unit
115 Ownership paper
116 Donald Duck's nephew
117 Shed tears

DOWN

1 Uses a straw
2 In ___ (stuck)
3 Western tie
4 Open
5 Having feeling
6 Dinosaur origin
7 Impetuous
8 Complete
9 Move smoothly
10 Age
11 Holiday drinks
12 Lend a hand
13 A violinist is always . . .
14 "Step ___!"
15 Part of SA
16 Bradwell or Breckinridge
22 Woes
23 Texas AFB
28 Mrs. Charles
30 Cornet inserts
32 Took a spill
34 London watering hole
35 Claire and Balin
36 Wall Street option
37 Christmas songs
39 In the neighborhood
40 Zero
41 Pulls
42 Spline
46 "Help!" director
49 A drummer might . . .
50 Filled with respect
51 Hammer, for one
53 Just purchased
57 West in "Klondike Annie"
59 Skillful
61 Four-poster
63 Thread reel
65 160 square rods
66 Abel's undoer
67 Green reptile, for short
68 Loco
70 Slumps
72 See 5 Across
73 Pizarro's conquest
76 Robby in "Salsa"
78 Move aside
79 Skip stones
81 FDR's mother
83 Wetland
87 Made a collar
89 On the tardy side
90 Knitter's need
91 Avoid
94 Acknowledged applause
96 TV's "___ Girl"
97 Take on
98 Raines in "Brute Force"
99 Nobelist Metchnikoff
101 Son of Isaac
103 Depression
104 Pennsylvania city
105 Break apart
108 Cuprite, for one
109 "___ to Joy"

35 ARTS AND CRAFTS   by Kenneth Haxton
Names in the arts result in a very crafty construction.

ACROSS

1 Elec. unit
4 "___ well that ends . . ."
8 Truman's birthplace
13 Emulate Casca
17 Racer Wood
18 Bly or Merrill
19 Frog order
20 Cue for strings
21 Galena or bauxite
22 "Rule Britannia" composer
23 Wear the crown
24 Winningham in "One-Trick Pony"
25 Kidd or Laffite
27 "Sergeant York" star
29 "The Mary Tyler Moore Show" producer
32 Glen Gray and his Casa ___ Orchestra
33 Like yttrium
34 Maxwell or Lancaster
35 Desiccated
36 "Sweeney Agonistes" auth.
39 Sampras and Graf, often
41 One of Alcott's women
44 Lecherous
46 Connecticut Maritime Museum site
48 "Adagio for Strings" composer
51 Mammoth or Lascaux
53 Elated
54 Away from the wind
55 Geodesic dome inventor
60 Assam silkworm
61 "GoodFellas" star
62 Meeny preceder
63 "McCloud" star
66 Akin to clannish
71 1066 and 1492
72 Hot
73 Worship
74 Alias
75 "Drink to the ___": Sheridan
78 Location of Nod from Eden
82 Raines in "Uncle Harry"
83 "Champagne Tony" of golf
84 "The Goodbye Girl" star
87 "Private Dancer" singer
91 Most robust
92 Litmus reddener
93 Bessemer product
94 Theaters
95 Baseball stat
98 Painter Magritte
99 Expunge
100 Cleave
101 Lowe in "Masquer-ade"
102 Breslau river
103 Gets rid of
104 Art deco designer
105 Address abbr.

DOWN

1 Yore
2 Deface
3 Readies
4 Disparate
5 Ligulate
6 Hardy soup
7 "Village Wedding" and "Skittle Players"
8 Elephantine
9 Close to
10 Glacier of Alaska
11 Sock pattern
12 Venom
13 Navigator Islands now
14 Football play
15 Rio Branco's state
16 Jan Smuts, for one
26 Like argon
28 Alpha's opposite
29 Sword of Sigmund
30 Blue
31 Shrine in Mecca
35 "The Red Shoes" star
36 Put aside a motion
37 Guide
38 Painter Crowe
40 Under the weather
42 Theatrical
43 Adjust the pitch
45 Ph.D. exam
47 Bivouacs
48 Judo instructors
49 Luce publication
50 Burden
52 Forster's room had one
55 Rest period
56 Utah river
57 "Mondo ___" (1963)
58 Cicatrix
59 Vega's constellation
60 Icelandic epic
64 Dot in the drink
65 Fulda tributary
67 Comic strip lightbulbs
68 Reinforces
69 "Alice's Restaurant" singer
70 "Bridge on the River Kwai" director
76 What Queen Victoria was not
77 "No Exit" playwright
79 On the beach
80 Cap bill, for example
81 Aptitude
83 Cargo man
84 Former attorney general
85 Favorite spot of Van Gogh
86 Union general
87 Eddo
88 Frozen
89 Ennead number
90 "Bullets Over Broadway" heroine
96 Baloney!
97 Saperstein of basketball

36 COLD-BLOODED by Sam Bellotto Jr.
Your local reptilium may be helpful with solving this one.

ACROSS

1 "___ Again": Gershwin
5 Cervine male
9 Bash into
12 Register key
17 Choreographer White
18 Man-of-the-Year magazine
19 ___ Jima
20 Sky blue
21 "Boxing Helena" star
22 Novelist Sillitoe
23 Needlefish
24 Computer language
25 Slight hoarseness
29 "Fantasy Island" mermaid
30 Williams in "American Graffiti"
31 Take a second SAT
32 Winged: Comb. form
33 Preppy wear
35 Jane or John
36 Inventor Thomson
38 Painter Estienne
39 Barflies
44 However
45 Thick-soled sandals
47 Nonecclesiastical
48 "Marriage is ___ so grave": Stevenson
49 Small porch
50 "___ So Fine": Chiffons
51 Circuit component
52 Mr. Ed's family
55 Dice throw
59 Ruby and cardinal
60 Wake-up call?
62 Strain
63 Needles
65 Paramecium propeller
66 Masquerade
67 Untamed
68 Small island
71 British baked sausage dish
74 Twin
76 "Haystacks" painter
77 Baggage tag for O'Hare
78 He sang "Venus"
79 Prima donna
81 Capital of Punjab
84 White poplar
85 Aleta's son
86 Tool with serrated jaws
90 German spa
92 Neither Rep. nor Dem.
93 Madame Bovary
94 Baldwin in "Bad Guys"
95 Triton's milieu
96 Scrabble 2-pointer
97 Ransack
98 Tropical tuber
99 ___ cotta
100 ID on a 1040
101 Garret
102 Times to remember

DOWN

1 Tip one's hat
2 Humdinger
3 Sinless
4 Moroccan seaport
5 Bleachers
6 Sloping
7 Rajah's governess
8 Unlike Scrooge
9 Might often makes this
10 Sentient
11 Full of gloom and doom
12 ___-Hartley Act
13 Word form of "smell"
14 Capsize
15 George Ade book
16 "The Land of Smiles" composer
26 Charge with an offense
27 Summer job-seeker
28 Hun king
32 "Star Trek" weapons
33 Quaker pronoun
34 Itsy-bitsy
35 Home of the Yokums
37 North African dress
39 Bird on a Canadian coin
40 Joviality
41 "And this her ___ imprisonment . . .": Shak.
42 Pushing up daisies
43 Sutherland-Gould film
46 ___ Alamos
49 Creaking sound
50 Put a spell on
52 Guarantee
53 Hodgepodge
54 Oven for glazing food
56 Capshaw in "Just Cause"
57 Literary governess
58 Karlovy Vary, e.g.
61 Popular street name
64 Stone or Reed
66 Kings of Pergamum
67 Look into the future
68 Ordo, for one
69 "Long ___ and Far Away": Taylor
70 Thousand rin
72 Jodie Foster role
73 Romanian round dance
75 Synthetic resin ester
78 CGS unit of electrical power
79 French footwear
80 Harness strap
82 "Running Scared" star
83 Publisher Reid
84 Long ___ the law
86 Early Beatles song
87 "Typee" sequel
88 "Fame" name
89 Med. ins. plans
91 Attentiveness

37 BEEP! BEEP! by Raymond Hamel
Here's a little taxonomy lesson from Warner Bros.

ACROSS

1 Render replete
5 Storms
10 Made a chess move
17 Actress Louise
19 Siskel's partner
20 Document holder
21 Relished
22 "Gloria ___"
23 Nuptial
24 Road Runner in "Zoom and Bored" (1957)
27 Superman's adopted home
28 Fat farms
29 Tolkien's ringbearer
33 Entrepreneur's org.
36 Explorer from Orkney
37 Told tales
39 Coming up
40 Road Runner in "Scrambled Aches" (1957)
46 Vicinity
47 Golden apple tosser
48 Temperament
49 Texas statesman
51 Auctioneer's word
52 Key and Knight
54 Snorkel or Preston
55 Wile E. Coyote in "Gee Whiz-z-z" (1956)
59 FDR agcy.
62 Pier percher
63 Sales warning
64 "Full House" star
68 Starting point
70 Declaration of innocence
71 "The ___ of Spring": Stravinsky
72 Road Runner in "Guided Muscle" (1955)
78 Distance runner Zatopek
79 Dyed rabbit fur
80 Mex. matron
81 Small part
82 Tries for a part
84 Column width measure
86 Early video-game name
88 Wile E. Coyote in "Ready, Set, Zoom" (1955)
94 Sea anemone
97 Turn of a phrase
98 Gounod opera
99 Rocket type
100 High clouds
101 Mock
102 Dollar figure
103 "Woman Undressing" painter
104 Complain

DOWN

1 Swedish car
2 One against
3 Layer
4 Study piece
5 Good names
6 Disconcert
7 Stan of the sax
8 "To ___ human . . ."
9 Paints with points
10 Light shirts
11 Burnoose wearer
12 Bench warmer
13 "The Bugs Bunny/Road Runner Hour" theme song
14 Started the grill
15 Mrs. Jerome Kern
16 Singer Shannon
18 Birdhouse
25 Berlin beer
26 Opener, perhaps
30 Center
31 French market town
32 Beginning
33 Unpartnered
34 Dave of the PGA
35 On the QE2
38 Orphan of comics
41 Not spicy
42 Kim Young Sam's capital
43 Coffeehouse equipment
44 Pinto
45 Roman nose
50 Orlando team
51 Evans of jazz
52 Kind of run
53 Wynn and Harris
56 Loose, draped gown
57 ". . . dagger ___ before me?": Shak.
58 Madras wrap
59 Book jacket
60 ___ de menthe
61 Eyelashes
65 "Shadow Dancing" singer
66 Toiletries case
67 Final
69 Geppetto's Cleo, e.g.
70 Dionne Warwick's friends
73 Edward Scissorhands' talent
74 Les Etats-___
75 Worsted fabric
76 Review at the last minute
77 Import duty
83 ___ Domingo
85 Check the books
86 Mentioned leader
87 Shorthand inventor Pitman
89 Outward appearance
90 Palomino parent
91 Storytelling dance
92 Superpower of yore
93 Aerobics prop
94 Asimov's "Murder at the ___"
95 Take in
96 Small fry

38 TRAILBLAZERS by Robert Zimmerman
A 19th-century feminist cause can be found at 39 Down.

ACROSS

1 Gave up
6 Disconcert
11 Indian prince
16 Tempts
18 Limbaugh's medium
19 Mistreat
20 Advocate of 39 Down
22 Oscar's roommate
23 Author Ludwig
24 "Ah, me!"
25 Kindled again
27 Chemical suffix
28 Mandrill, e.g.
29 One of AA's 12
30 Burdened
31 Fannie and Daisy
32 Grand ___ Opry
33 Suspect's excuse
35 Pulled
37 Sentimental to a fault
41 Shore feature
43 Use art gum
46 Skirt around
47 Foch's force
49 Peach variety
51 Weighty volume
52 Cuss
53 Algonquian
54 ___ Moines
55 Jet insignia
56 Makes pumpernickel
57 Shade of pink
58 Magician's prop
59 Chinese dynasty
60 Composer Satie
61 Dyed fabric
62 Colosseum site
63 Loser
65 Blender setting
66 High rise
67 Customary
68 Fright
70 Directories
72 Guitar ridge
74 Wash cycle
76 Stadium echo
77 Sandy's greetings
79 Player's rep
81 Hideout
83 Ad ___
86 Disfigure
87 Brisling
88 Granary
89 Poor boy
90 Edict
92 Advocate of 39 Down
95 Make a transition
96 Danger
97 Wind-borne
98 Utopias
99 Ford heir
100 Lay out

DOWN

1 Grass cluster
2 "The Prince and the Showgirl" heroine
3 For two
4 Sea bird
5 Campaign events
6 Some are fine
7 "Humbug!"
8 Charming
9 Adjournment team
10 Game expert
11 Kon Tiki, e.g.
12 Novelist Kobo
13 Advocate of 39 Down
14 Parenthetical remark
15 Spells
16 On a cruise
17 Mall attraction
21 Wine valley
26 Ill. neighbor
29 Used a sled
30 LP jacket
31 Nothing more than
32 Dust Bowl migrant
34 Beans
36 Recalcitrant
37 "Grumpier Old Men" star
38 Admissions
39 Amendment XIX concern
40 Sadie ___ Day
42 Wirehair
44 Stanley ___
45 Spring holidays
48 Fume
50 Ooze out
52 Actress Allgood
53 D'Azur
56 Pioneer TV comic
57 Solicitudes
61 Blackened
62 "Zuckerman Unbound" author
64 Shell movers
65 Bonheur and Bonnard
66 Romanov title
69 Trounced
71 Camden Yards team
73 Gregory Hines specialty
75 "The Supernatural Man" essayist
77 Entertain
78 Gathered leaves
80 Wine, figuratively
82 Duchess of ___
83 Surround
84 Mountain nymph
85 Golden bantam, for one
87 Bishoprics
88 Window ledge
89 "Fixing a ___": Beatles
91 Energy source
93 Fib
94 Alley of the comics

ACROSS

1 Moan and groan
5 Elite police unit
9 Attire for Galahad
13 Tucker
17 Wing-shaped
18 Henry VIII's sixth
19 "___ la Douce" (1963)
20 Letters on a Sydney ship
21 Green fee?
22 Part of ADL
23 Repeat offender
25 WHO
28 Edsel had an odd one
29 Mary ___ Place
30 On the road: Abbr.
31 Where Bourg is
32 Potatoes au ___
35 "Speed" setting
37 Daytona event
41 Shankar specialty
43 Rapping Dr.
44 Stand-up standards
45 Commotions
46 WHAT
51 Insulation fiberboard
54 Slangy turndown
55 Persona's opposite
56 Nile reptile
57 "___ to Pieces": Cline
58 Formicarian
59 Thumbs up, in space
61 One in a Thousand Islands
62 Piglet
64 "___ he drove out of sight . . ."
65 NATO or SEATO
67 WHERE
71 Once (upon a time)
72 Hors d'oeuvre selection
73 Latin 201
74 "Cotton Candy" trumpeter
78 Pere David's ___
79 Part of LPGA
80 Starr reporter
83 Conservative leader
84 "Deep Space Nine" officer
86 Spanish Main cargo
87 Palestinian Nobelist
89 WHEN
96 Like caconyms
97 Sarcophagus
98 Remus Rabbit
100 Poet Asnyk
101 Rose or Lily
102 Nice notion
103 Spa near Palermo
104 Service-station job
105 Counterfeit-er's nemesis
106 What Barnard College is not
107 Badgered

DOWN

1 Airline-governing agcy.
2 Barbary Coast country
3 Freebooter's forte
4 Nose around
5 Less fatty
6 Dorati's stick
7 Some are fine
8 Better at swindling
9 "All ___ were the borogoves": Carroll
10 Onassis and namesakes
11 "___ Lonesome I Could Cry"
12 Native American game
13 Ellington's "Take ___"
14 Somalian model
15 "The Fountainhead" author
16 Small appraisals
24 Plato's P
26 Math. course
27 McShane in "Lovejoy"
28 Needlefish
33 Supplement
34 Tulip ___
35 Avon spa
36 "How gross!"
38 "The Boy Friend" actor
39 Vast
40 Manderly or Brideshead
42 Latin conjugation starter
44 British mosquito
47 Cry from a labor organizer
48 Apparatus
49 Tube type
50 Moslem mendicant
51 Pulverized
52 On liberty
53 Significant other
58 Johnson of "Laugh-In"
59 Food thickener
60 "___ Buttermilk Sky"
63 Houston stadium
64 End of Missouri's motto
65 Utter finish
66 ___ Can School
68 Apollo Creed, to Rocky
69 Wide partner
70 Crossword cousin
75 Hellish place
76 Backside
77 Rugrat
80 Lingerie item
81 Smeared
82 Radius location
85 Secluded room
86 Sportscaster Merlin
88 Source of dinosaur DNA
89 Naval commando
90 Pakistani tongue
91 Uninteresting
92 Good earth
93 Arizona city
94 Kind of list
95 "Jolly Roger" crewman
99 Tommy Chong's daughter

ACROSS

1 "Madcap Maxie"
5 Complete catastrophe
11 "Big" boys
17 Novelist Lagerlof
18 Remove from a wagon
19 Author Christie
20 How 54 Across rubbed it in?
23 Bend forward to hear
24 "___ Believer": Monkees
25 AAA suggestion
26 "Lady and the Tramp" dog
27 What 54 Across drove on?
32 Game-show big prizes
35 Somalia's gulf
36 Naturalization org.
37 John in "Missing"
40 Paul's "Exodus" role
41 Wroclaw's river
42 Mid-alphabet letter
43 Work like ___
45 Indigenes
47 Demote
49 Floral necklace
50 Put down
51 Chess champ Mikhail
52 "I cannot ___ . . .": Washington
54 Figurehead?
58 Bandage
61 Randolph of labor
62 Town near Amiens
66 Once-called
67 Spherical
69 In the group
71 Colleen
73 Secret ending
74 ___ example
75 Ad ___
76 Skewer
77 Census info
78 Group of toads
79 River into the Seine
80 Took away, to 54 Across
85 "Star Trek: DS9" character
87 Louis XIII or XIV
88 UK defenders
89 Kind of play
93 What 54 Across did his work on?
98 For each one
99 It has a B-side
100 Deck out
101 More bloodshot
102 English economist
103 Twinge

DOWN

1 George Eliot hero
2 Soprano Frances
3 Fixes up
4 Arm bones
5 Jollity
6 One in the know
7 Clear-sightedness
8 Dieter's lunch
9 Office monitor
10 Hubbell's roommate
11 Country singer Hill
12 Ford replaced him
13 ___ Mahal
14 Period for homework
15 German-Czech river
16 Vocalizes
17 "Erie Canal" mule
21 Swarm over
22 Assns.
28 Midmonth date
29 Hotfoots it
30 Laziness
31 Tray filler
32 Where water turned to wine
33 Bedouin
34 Actress Tushingham
38 ". . . ___ saw Elba"
39 Friendly femme
41 Surplus amount
42 Having an umbrella-like cap
43 King in the "Volsunga Saga"
44 Very pale blue
46 "___ Mommy Kissing Santa Claus"
47 Hoover or Kariba
48 DOE's predecessor
51 Queens racetrack, familiarly
53 Shortly
55 "___ do for now"
56 Le Duc ___
57 "Marina" poet: Init.
58 They justify the means
59 Half-moon tide
60 Gelatin, e.g.
63 Wrinkly fruit
64 Unfixed
65 "Let ___": Beatles
68 With, to Rene
69 Beginning
70 Prison supervisor
72 Before V
74 Rock's Earth, Wind ___
77 Nutmeg covering
78 "Annie Hall" actress
79 Golfer Mark
81 Fanny of vaudeville
82 Imbiber
83 Singer Chapman
84 Available
85 Sheik Abdel-Rahman
86 Hoodwink
90 Hillside shelter
91 Clique
92 "Brat Farrar" author
94 Schroeder of tennis
95 Tick off
96 Middling mark
97 "___ bodkins!"

41 CHASING THE BLUES   by Deborah Trombley
Want another colorful puzzle?

ACROSS

1 G-men
5 "The Alphabet Song" beginning
9 Guy counterpart
12 Ring bearer?
16 Secular
17 Pop that gets drunk
18 Route of passage
20 Noggin
21 Singer Guthrie
22 3600 seconds
23 Grimm's uxoricide
25 Vinton hit of 1963
28 Land markers
29 Car of old
30 Influential contacts
31 Ward heelers
32 Gloss
35 Sea bird
37 Rodgers & Hart song
41 One of 52
42 Smelting residue
43 Sounds of despair
44 Chinese principle
45 Start of a Faulkner title
46 Straightforward
47 "___ something I said?"
48 Glove worn by Bench
49 Wambaugh novel
52 Sheriff's band
53 Annex
54 Egg: Comb. form
55 Pact of 1948
56 Prayer endings
59 Microsoft, to investors
66 Appraise
67 Connery and Penn
68 Onassis and namesakes
69 Skater Babilonia
70 Pop or Op follower
71 Tiffs
72 Ballet move
73 Female deer
74 African river
76 "Malle Babbe" painter
77 Sped
78 Extra
79 Fool
80 So-so score for Norman
81 Spanish explorer
84 Peppard film
89 Kind of special
92 Uncle Scar's outburst
93 Stowe's "The Pearl of ___ Island
95 Deceiver
96 Blackthorn
97 Nephew of Abel
98 Like some misses
99 Irwin and Udall
100 Directed
101 Two aspirin, usually
102 Walk-the-dog toy

DOWN

1 Pie ___ mode
2 Duds
3 Register
4 Scrubbed
5 Allergic reaction
6 Blessing
7 Cudgel
8 Julie Christie film
9 Taunts
10 Me. neighbor
11 Romanian coin
12 Belief in Him
13 Bring up
14 Merit
15 Adv. degrees
19 Election loser's demand
24 Bundles
26 Poetic contraction
27 One, on the Seine
31 Interweave
32 Word for a stray
33 Hodgepodge
34 Pennsylvania city
35 Robert on Traveler
36 Seeding
37 "Rubbish!"
38 He had his ups and downs?
39 Filly filler
40 Middle C, for one
42 It has eyes but can't see
43 Prestidigitation
46 Auto pioneer
47 Victims of 23 Across
48 Majority
50 Curse
51 Gerunds
52 Annie Oakley
55 Mayberry moppet
56 Riyadh resident
57 City in the Ruhr Valley
58 Words of accusation
59 Baldwin's "If ___ Street Could Talk"
60 Like the White Rabbit
61 "High Adventure" author
62 Water flag
63 Auricular
64 Sugar, for one
65 "The Wizard of the Sea"
67 Helixes
71 Pry
72 Covered the walls
73 Synch
75 Coals
76 "I don't believe it!"
77 Actress Dawn Chong
79 Horse
80 Bag
81 OPEC units
82 Landed
83 Hawaiian feast
85 "Hairspray" star
86 Landlocked land
87 Mars: Comb. form
88 Roentgen discovery
90 Jack-of-___-trades
91 Nursery "piggy"
94 Socko sign

42

HOW ABOUT SOME MUSIC?   by Raymond Hamel
A quartet of hits with a common connection.

ACROSS

1 "Charlie's Angels" star
5 Ray Palmer's secret identity
9 Indonesian island
13 Thick slice
17 Mimic
18 Fuddy-duddy
19 Yoke carriers
20 Howland Owl's pal
21 Grand Funk Railroad hit
25 "Pocahontas" producer
26 Bankruptcy
27 Together
28 Trifle
29 Father
30 Chieftain's concern
31 Look for
34 Coq au ___
35 Slump
36 He defeated Tunney
40 Olivia Newton-John hit
45 Swear
46 Enzyme ending
47 God of love
48 Winter, in Cannes
49 Ballpoint
50 Skiing maneuver
52 Second
53 God with iron gloves
54 Antiquity
55 Gnu feature
56 John Wayne film
59 Estrange
61 Fashion line
64 Open-eyed
65 Where the pot gets hot
66 Feign
67 Pleasant
68 Barry Manilow hit
72 Entreaty
73 None in particular
74 Giant of a Giant
75 D'Artagnan companion
76 Oates of the NFL
78 Piece of cake
80 Ex-Knick Louis
81 Decorates
84 Cabbage variety
85 Author Welty
88 McGuire Sisters hit
92 Israeli dance
93 Pernicious
94 Baxter or Bancroft
95 Collar style
96 Actor Estrada
97 Astrolabe plate
98 Fiscal ___
99 Hawaiian honker

DOWN

1 "Viva ___ Vegas" (1964)
2 An amoeba, for instance
3 Moore in "Disclosure"
4 More like Beau Brummel
5 Tours "ta-ta"
6 Award named after Perry
7 Leftover
8 Dock action
9 Knife inventor
10 Neural transmitter
11 Writer Deighton
12 Participate
13 When robins return
14 Attic
15 Fever
16 Valorous
22 Kentucky county
23 Pelisse lining
24 She reigned in Spain
29 Muscle
30 Birman and Siamese
31 Pronto, briefly
32 Used the loom
33 Congregational response
34 Poker wear
35 Hide
37 Wander
38 "Flaming Star" star
39 Low-quality diamond
41 Vietnamese city
42 "St. Mark Preaching in Alexandria" painter
43 Wear down
44 Avignon's river
50 Mole relative
51 "___ the Conqueror" (1988)
52 Rough finish
53 Rest
55 "Nightwing" actor
56 Fastener
57 Wayward GI
58 Not spicy
59 Light
60 Fashionable
61 Pricy
62 Reverberation
63 Shea nine
65 Slugger Hrbek
67 It's most of the air
69 More abrasive
70 Small bouquet
71 "Mandrake" foe
77 Hill worker
78 "Fly Like an ___": Steve Miller Band
79 Michaels and Kaline
80 On the perimeter
81 Court great
82 Entrance
83 Ahab's father
84 Needle, in a way
85 Sicilian spewer
86 Bas mitzvah, e.g.
87 Bard's river
89 "___ Got a Secret"
90 "A Chorus Line" finale
91 Buffalo-Syracuse dir.

43 CREATURE DOUBLE FEATURE by Joel D. Lafargue
Punful clues lead to creatures that really exist.

ACROSS

1 Protrude (out)
4 Cotton on a stick
8 Proper partner
12 "George of the Jungle" elephant
16 "Regretful" miss
18 Take on
19 "Ta-___-Boom-De-Ré"
20 Epitaph beginning
21 Part of baby's vocabulary
22 Sommer in "Zeppelin"
23 Arabian Sea nation
24 Seine feeder
25 She created a Frankenstein
27 ONE CLEVER RODENT?
30 Lively time
31 Ethereal
32 Rubbish!
33 Confectioner's nut
35 Low grade
36 Anytime
41 Spanish province
42 Olfactory stimulus
44 Bus. firms
45 Where Moses died
46 "Spring ahead" abbr.
47 Ripening need
48 Game with ringers
51 Brady Bill opp.
52 Dumas dueler
54 Cessation
56 KING OF THE HILL?
58 Short road
60 Helped after dinner
62 Water tester
63 MORRIS ON THE WING?
67 Brother of Prometheus
69 Labyrinths
73 An eye for the senoritas?
74 Sewing-box item
76 Music to Seinfeld's ears
78 Old English letter
79 Astro or aqua follower
81 "Cry ___ River"
82 History Muse
83 Tony's cousin
84 Great lengths
87 ___ tai (cocktail)
88 Brought up
90 Baiul contemporary
91 Golfer Barrett
92 ___ precedent
93 SCOUNDREL WITH A POUCH?
98 Sake
101 Creative: Abbr.
102 "Cactus Flower" heroine
103 Hebrew letter
105 Bailiff's order
106 Do a November duty
107 Basso Pinza
108 Roger Williams hit
109 JFK arrivals
110 Washstand vessel
111 Meadowlands five
112 Sheedy in "WarGames"
113 One-third of a Buster Poindexter tune

DOWN

1 Runs through Central Park
2 Bryce Canyon site
3 LOVER OF STRIPED CLOTHES?
4 WOOLLY WOOFER?
5 Cunning
6 Tenn. neighbor
7 More muscular
8 Placeholder
9 St. Louis eleven
10 Hussein's land
11 Organic fertilizer
12 Truncate
13 Hand-me-down recipient?
14 Celtic tongue
15 Steed's companion
17 The Long Branch was one
26 K–O go-betweens
28 Tram contents
29 End of a quest?
31 Thought the world of
33 "Same Time, Next Year" actor
34 "___ we forget . . ."
36 It can be pitched
37 First Chinese dynasty
38 Part of Caesar's declaration
39 River in Aragon province
40 Bookbinding leather
43 The ___ Vikings ('50s group)
44 Assayer's vessel
47 The Riddler, before Carey
48 Very
49 Turner network
50 Small leaf opening
53 Sphere
55 Lilting refrain
57 Thompson in "Nightbreaker"
59 Before, to Browning
61 Ball-shaped flower
63 Cotton-candy holder
64 Trojan War hero
65 "I've-got-a-horse-for-you" guy
66 Hellenic township
68 Long-tailed monkey
70 SEA LION'S PREY?
71 Newscaster Magnus
72 Take off pounds
75 Actor Michael ___ Barres
77 BUGBOY'S MOUNT?
80 Famous palomino
82 "Wachet auf," e.g.
83 Lash La Rue pictures
85 Fraternity letter
86 Placekicker Andersen
87 Actress Sara
89 Dusk, to Donne
91 Kingston et al.
93 Martin of "Cagney and Lacey"
94 Lined up
95 "Rock On" author
96 Seep through
97 "Let's shake ___!"
98 Pepper type
99 Comparison words
100 Dry run
104 Small form of "small"

44 SCIENCE LESSON by Ernest Lampert
A clever first-time offering from a San Franciscan doctor.

ACROSS

1 Dawn
7 Clerical wear
12 Grades
17 Nickname
18 Future seed
19 Transistors
21 **Science lesson: Part I**
25 Dir.
26 "Swan Lake" role
27 Ready for picking
28 Caliber
29 Hebrew month
31 Scorns
33 Undiluted
35 Dial on the dash
36 Bathed gently
38 Ger.
39 "The Mill on the Floss" author
42 Conservative beginning
43 Tower of 110 stories
45 Apothecary's dispensations
48 Redactors
50 Problem at the CIA
52 Trig function
53 Lever
54 Storm preceder
57 "My country, ___ . . ."
59 Word form of "sound"
61 Trapper
65 Ring king
66 Heir's relative
68 Proficient
70 Caroline, to Ted
71 **Science lesson: Part II**
75 Contact via Internet
76 Kind of statement
77 Teases
78 Race the engine
79 Punched
81 Fugard title plants
83 Apprehend
84 Give a darn
85 Arabian prince
87 School test
89 Olekma's end
91 Ornithologist
94 Consequence
95 Dithers and Witherspoon
98 Path: Suffix
99 Enhance
101 Hats for MacDougal
104 Displaced
106 ___ Bator
108 Average
110 Heather
112 Muskeg
113 Counseled: Brit.
115 Period of service
117 Aromas
119 Diego's day
120 **Science lesson: Part III**
125 Hard money
126 Fred Astaire's sister
127 Stimulus
128 Williams in "Smooth Talk"
129 Wanders
130 Gauges

DOWN

1 Politicians have them
2 Disentangle
3 Balderdash!
4 Melville novel
5 Splits
6 Apply pomade
7 "Gather ye ___ while . . .": Herrick
8 First or Second
9 Trilling sound
10 Singing chipmunk
11 Homes on the range
12 Mrs., in Managua
13 Malibu hue
14 Dutch cheese
15 Lab tube
16 Marilyn Horne, e.g.
17 Yearly record
20 Deli appliance
22 "NYPD ___"
23 Truman's was Fair
24 Group character
30 Demesne
32 Emulate Gypsy Rose Lee
34 Level
37 Rapping Dr.
40 Of a lyric poem
41 Medicinal teas
44 "Little Miss Muffet ___ . . ."
46 Stable a horse
47 Crystal-lined rock
49 Lackadaisical
51 NBA team
53 Cotton material
54 Sidewalk eateries
55 San Antonio bowl
56 Pale purple
58 Naval conflict
60 Intimate
62 Neon fish
63 Earth pigment
64 "Somewhere in Time" star
66 Quandary
67 Organic compound
69 Type of wave
72 Took a fancy to
73 What a butterfingers does
74 Mediterranean vessel
80 Extinct
82 Pan-fry
84 Handball bounce
86 He lived 905 years
88 Fragrant flowers
90 ___ de guerre
91 French market town
92 Wastrels
93 Adjust to new circumstances
94 To such an extent
96 Eagerness
97 Yahoo in "Young Einstein"
100 Magazine section
102 Haydn symphony
103 Nova ___
105 Acheson and Jagger
107 On no account
109 Go one better
111 Calla lilies
114 One of the Horae
116 Sister of Cronus
118 Dumb clucks
121 Castilian aunt
122 Nevertheless
123 Arboreal street name
124 Actress Leoni

45 IT WAS A VERY GOOD YEAR   by William Canine
Many of us still have fond memories of that time.

ACROSS

1 Cleaned up
6 Onager
9 Round ammo
12 Bargain
18 Williams heroine
19 Kinshasha citizen
21 Phantasmal
22 Kansas prohibitionist
23 Pyrenees republic
24 Red-brown
25 "Vissi d'___": Puccini
26 Emmy winner: 1986
29 Painter Bernini
30 America's Cup team
31 Attribute
32 Culbertson
33 Aromatic ointment
34 Part of the Mass
36 NBA MVP: 1986
42 First Family in 1846
43 Prof. Rhine's specialty
45 Medicine men
46 Comparative ending
47 Cascade peak
50 Florida city
51 Seductresses
54 Ponder
55 City NE of Venice
58 Soul
61 "Dear me!"
63 Disturb
64 Steamship
65 City on the Meuse
66 Scruff
67 Cooper's tool
68 Droop
69 Addition
70 Batting champ Raines:1986
71 "American Gothic" artist
73 Relative perforce
76 Dishonor
78 Haiku, for one
79 Solitary
80 Thornburgh's predecessor
81 Accipitrine feature

82 Excellent
83 ___ Domingo
85 Neighbor of Dartmund
87 Intimidates
89 Forefront
90 "Norma" composer
92 "Diamond ___"
93 Viper
96 Derby winner: 1986
98 Weasel
102 Lacerate
103 Iranian river
104 Undemo-cratic?
106 She outwrestled Thor
107 Lucerne
108 World Series champs: 1986
114 Parapet
115 Songlike
117 Marianas, e.g.
118 Deodorant target
120 Nap
121 Jacqueline du Pré, e.g.
122 Contracts
123 Tepee-shaped
124 Malayan isthmus
125 Ginseng or rose hip
126 Persian prophet

DOWN

1 Like Taurus
2 Not as dry
3 Peace Nobelist: 1986
4 Arafat's acronym
5 Brando's last one was in Paris
6 Spring bloomers
7 Chopin paramour
8 Aspect
9 "Wozzeck" composer
10 City E of Naples
11 Trappers

12 Minx
13 Puzzler's cuckoo
14 British Open champ: 1986
15 Kindly
16 Scottish county
17 Antelopes
18 In-between meal
20 Hextall or Howard
27 Pussycat's partner
28 Legal-eagle's degree
35 Superlative ending
37 Lyon's river
38 Formula One vehicle
39 Soprano Sumac
40 Spinel
41 Insipid
42 A legume
44 Grammy winner: 1986
46 U.S. Open champ: 1986

47 Loll
48 Jinxes
49 NCAA baseball champs: 1986
52 Best Picture winner: 1986
53 Wise
56 Sam Malone's old flame
57 Fireplace
59 Utopian
60 Swedish seaport
62 Confederate general
72 Pulitzer winning newspaper: 1986
74 Interrogator
75 Wooded country
76 Woodland
77 Barbera's partner
78 Oscar-winning actor: 1986
84 Cigarette component

86 Year in Leo IX's reign
88 Sloths
90 Wilkes-Barre neighbor
91 Hay, in the rumen
93 Finally
94 Merman-Bolger hit
95 Belgian saint
96 Antagonist
97 Flyspeck
99 Pass
100 Supporters
101 Pleated skirts
103 Work clay
105 Hymn
109 North Sea feeder
110 Jug
111 NC capital: Abbr.
112 Furrow
113 Goods: Abbr.
116 ___ Anne de Beaupré
119 "Citizen X" star

YORE HIT PARADE   by Roger H. Courtney
Stars of the past light up the squares below.

ACROSS

1 Coffer
6 Marginal marks
11 Streetcar in Sheffield
15 Gaelic
19 Derry demolisher
20 ___ Haute
21 ___ avis
22 Holidays in Hanoi
23 Nolan Ryan was one
24 Sigourney Weaver film
25 Rat-___
26 Tropical trees
27 Winning Las Vegas group?
29 Call for hamburger?
31 Letter letters
32 Little troublemaker
34 Boxcars - 1
35 Tracks
39 Dance for Cugat
42 43,560 square feet
44 Suffix for computer
45 Probity
46 Tests to cram for
47 Group for Earp
49 Aleutian island
50 Crafty musician?
52 "What a pity!"
56 Contaminate
58 "The Third Man" director
59 Dumbo's are jumbo
60 Met exclamation
61 Early Yale president
63 "What's ___ for me?"
64 "___ down the hatches!"
65 Formed a sphere
67 Ara, for one
69 Rules of conduct
70 Chompers
71 Litigates
72 Disheveled
74 Gather
75 "___ boy!"
76 ___ fide
78 Crossbones' companion
81 Congregation of the Oratory founder
82 Singer on the beam?
84 ___ fixe
85 Type of grease
88 Grandmas, at times
89 Office worker
90 Outdoors-man's org.
93 Priestly vestments
94 Adversary
95 Nigel Bruce role
96 City on the Rio Grande
98 Robinson or Doubtfire
99 Gift of ___
100 Lake crooner?
103 Sings for the "halibut?"
111 Puzzled
112 D.W. Griffith subject
113 Approaches
114 Herman's Hermit
115 Mama or Peggy
116 Nobelist Wiesel
117 Nasser's follower
118 Matriarch of "Dallas"
119 Funnyman Johnson
120 Carry on
121 Uneven
122 Stones

DOWN

1 With demo or auto
2 Corned-beef dish
3 Italian city S of Padua
4 Helot
5 Mountie
6 Walk-of-Fame sights
7 Honduran seaport
8 Stoltz in "Rob Roy"
9 Bonsai or banyan
10 Intelligent
11 "Sound of Music" family
12 Pro ___
13 Smell -___
14 "Family ___": TV sitcom
15 Storehouse
16 Macadamize again
17 Phases
18 Palestinian ascetic
28 Pkg. shippers
30 French islands
33 City on the St. Lawrence
35 "Who's ___ Girl": Madonna
36 "The Godfather Theme" composer
37 Opposite the sun
38 Royal swinger?
39 Lords
40 Type of room
41 Marian
42 In pieces
43 Cud chewers
46 ___-thee-well
48 Geologist's luggage?
51 "Easy To Be Hard" musical
53 Liberties
54 ___ plaisir
55 Steve Douglas had three
57 Anagram for rites
60 Psycho in "Psycho"
62 Mormons: Abbr.
63 "___ Howdy Doody time . . ."
64 One of the Cartwrights
65 Hoover was one
66 Capital of Togo
67 Small pen?
68 Love of Hero
71 Puts in the hold
72 Mathematical function
73 Certain votes
75 "Get ___": 1958 hit
76 Computer unit
77 Utah city
79 Carson's successor
80 Biographer Edel
83 "Horsefeathers!"
86 ___-in-waiting
87 Halfback's helper
89 Conquered people of 290 B.C.
90 Bolivian wool
91 Lover of Cleopatra
92 Seizure
95 WW2 servicewoman
97 Eliminate
98 "Poplars" painter
99 "Beau ___"
101 Spanish stew
102 Open ocean
104 Expensive
105 Part of a pedestal
106 Personal pension funds
107 One and only
108 Green cavity
109 Geraint's wife
110 Roger of "Cheers"

47 ADVICE TO GOLD DIGGERS by Betty Jorgensen
A humorous epigram from our Oregonian wit.

ACROSS

1 Cookbook words
4 High, to Henri
8 S.A. tropical forests
13 Luxurious
17 Hem length
19 Reporter on "Lou Grant"
20 Replica
21 Has an interest
22 Aboveboard
23 Bugged
24 Librarian's tool
25 Novelist Feuchtwanger
26 **Advice: Part I**
30 "___ with proclamations today": Shak.
33 Fruit protection
34 Biologic hand-me-downs?
35 Browsing the Internet
36 Dory driver
37 Enthusiasm
40 **Advice: Part II**
45 Shell game
49 Hamburg's river
50 Morrall of football
51 Vagabond
53 "This ___ House"
54 Ethiopian prince
55 Keach of "Mike Hammer"
57 He played Judge Hardy
59 Artist Kirchner
61 Blackbeard's real name
62 Unite
63 Practice pieces
64 **Advice: Part III**
69 City on the Oconee
70 Despise
71 All ___ Day
72 Pearls are cast before them
73 Appearances
75 He aims for the heart
76 USN officers
79 Ecru
80 Respond
82 Siamese
83 Delhi dress

84 On the bounding main
86 **Advice: Part IV**
91 Broadway boxes
93 Spleen
94 Will subject
95 Old Baltimore team
98 Irish islands
99 Seedless raisins
101 **Advice: Part V**
106 Bushy hairdo
107 Hydrophobic
108 Overly thin
109 Think tank thought
113 Nuremberg negative
114 Make up for
115 Lab burners
116 Metropolis
117 Killer whale
118 Molts
119 Korean soldiers
120 Wow!

DOWN

1 "Ti ___": Pavarotti album
2 Circuit
3 Fire
4 Tarpan, e.g.
5 Bid welcome
6 Operated
7 Sea anemone's home
8 Certain exam
9 Menotti title role
10 Hulot portrayer
11 Grows gray
12 Balkan native
13 Snitches
14 Cause of tears
15 Boutique
16 Whets
18 Harmonious
19 Car-wash mechanism
27 Geraldine's mom

28 Foster
29 Big "I am"
30 "Gaslight" actor
31 "Waterworld" girl
32 Dark suit
37 Prolific author
38 French illusion
39 Become a brunette
41 Arrive
42 Pleasure boat
43 Frizzle
44 Maine town
46 Publisher Nast
47 Oregon coastal town
48 New York nine
52 Emulated the Ancient Mariner
55 Net fisherman
56 Identifies
57 Classifies
58 Antler branch
60 Massages
61 Govt. agents

62 "Don ___ de Marco"
63 Compact case
64 "___ the best of times . . ."
65 "For ___ is the power . . ."
66 Between eta and iota
67 Common
68 Subject
69 Detective dog
73 Actress Winningham
74 Sews up
75 Chinese tea
76 Island nation
77 Garbo in "Anna Karenina"
78 Fathers
81 Golden-buck ingredient
82 One who thinks 30 is old

83 Fiendish
85 Pennsylvania city
87 Unpleasant lectures
88 Khaki
89 Thralls
90 Spanish pronoun
92 Covallis col.
95 Fascist statesman
96 Tender
97 Tuneful
98 "There's ___ of hush . . ."
99 Malodorous mammal
100 Arm bones
102 Ditty syllables
103 Swearword
104 Reed instrument
105 Defense org.
110 Get
111 After printemps
112 Yeoman's "yes"

48 FAMILY by Betty Jorgensen
As defined by a popular English playwright, Dodie Smith.

ACROSS

1 Abyss
6 Versed in
10 Bower
15 Mr. Universe's pride
18 Monster slain by Hercules
19 Byron poem
20 Get together
21 Chase flies
22 **Start of the definition**
26 Thing, to F. Lee Bailey
27 Bad March day
28 Sentence subject
29 Kelesi of tennis
30 Gaff
31 Steed steerers
33 Clarinet cousin
35 Cottonwoods
38 Custom
39 Alienated
44 Head iter
45 Half a train
46 Assuaged hunger
47 Nonprofessional
48 **More of the definition**
55 Lemnos letter
56 Commandment word
57 Digestive gland
58 Beneath
59 Cyclist Sorensen
61 Young rapscallion
62 Hoopster
63 Frame joints
64 WW2 vessels
66 Maitre d'___
67 Southwestern shrub
68 Coiffeur's quarters
71 Danger
72 Kind of jacket
73 Sweet talk
77 Miss America's crown
78 Connaught seaport
79 City of Ohio or Italy
81 ___ Altos
82 **More of the definition**
86 Stout
87 Rent
88 "It's ___ a paper moon . . ."
89 Ancient Greek region
90 Without compassion
94 Infuriates
95 Besmirches
96 Nonesuch
97 Hounds' quarry
99 Part of Dickens' signature
100 Odysseus' faithful dog
103 Silkworm
104 "Hoc ___ in votis"
105 P.I.
108 **End of the definition**
114 Be a partner in crime
115 Wear away
116 Coaster
117 Mitchell heroine
118 Dance, in Deauville
119 Peppery plate adornment
120 In addition
121 Certain post

DOWN

1 Cook Cajun-style
2 Park in London
3 Citrus coolers
4 Mrs., in Madrid
5 Tuliplike lilies
6 Tummy trouble
7 Riley and Robertson
8 Conquistador's quest
9 Short shut-eye
10 Flaming felony
11 Turn down
12 Ruin the toast
13 Yoko
14 Dreaming letters
15 MP's target
16 Low
17 Tommy's gun
21 Gloss
23 Harem hangouts
24 Part of a whole
25 Hippodrome command
30 Pornography
31 Perch
32 "Wilderness were Paradise ___": Khayyam
33 Trawler's board
34 ___ Rabbit
35 Word form of "star"
36 Ride out the storm
37 Historical record
38 Pup
40 Passbook possessor
41 Dance step
42 Trencherman
43 Some colorists
45 Money to Pal Joey
49 Café calculations
50 Bliss
51 Hawthorne or Bruce
52 First name in stunts
53 Call it a day
54 Up to
60 Fauna's partner
62 Queen Elizabeth's pet dog
63 Super Bowl XXIX site
65 Easy
66 Beneficiary
67 Toweling
68 Kind of heat
69 Bridal path
70 Shoe tier
71 Novelist's needs
72 St. ___ Cathedral, London
74 Massey in "Rosalie"
75 "Definitely not!"
76 These, in Toledo
78 Gibe
79 Cornbreads
80 Disney forte
83 "Vogue" rival
84 Long ago
85 Berg and Bandy
91 Woo
92 Part of M.I.T.
93 Makes confetti
94 Modern Mesopotamia
95 "Pygmalion" playwright
98 Buenos ___
99 Words to live by
100 Fictional whaler
101 Entertainer McEntire
102 Highlander
103 Satyr's shout
104 Saisons français
105 Lose your cool?
106 Very irregular French verb
107 Don't take this to Newcastle
109 Tiny time
110 Slip up
111 "Cartoon Express" network
112 Before wind or will
113 "___ Bop": Lauper hit

MISSING LINKS   by Nancy Nicholson Joline
A fill-in-the-blanks challenger from one of the best.

ACROSS

1 Grain dish
6 Anthony and Barbara
11 Meg Ryan film
14 Hoover's opponent: 1928
19 Rose oil
20 Narrator of a Chaucer tale
21 Sheffield loc.
22 Iraqi port
23 Mustard, ___, Supreme Court
25 Cocktail, ___, Rodgers and Hart
27 Kind of crab or snake
28 Coloratura Mills
29 Iago's wife
31 Charitable donations
32 Chevet
33 Raise
34 Durante's was famous
35 Nobelist Lech
37 Astrological butter
39 Rubbernecker
41 Thrilla-in-Manila winner
42 Apache, ___, paratrooper
47 Actor Kier of "Andy Warhol's Dracula"
48 Bermuda, ___, musical instrument
53 "___ I a woman?": Sojourner Truth
54 Three-syllable foot
57 Rhone tributary
58 Kind of pocket
59 Penultimate Greek letter
60 Amphora feature
62 Occasional dummy
64 Genoese magistrates
66 Karate instructor
68 Screenwriter Diamond
69 Afrikaner
71 He published "Glamour"
72 Disney World, ___, Virginia Woolf
74 Mt. Everest, ___, Clinton
76 Columnist Maureen
79 Pung, for one
80 Rough-country conveyance, for short
81 Burdensome
85 An artery
87 Like
89 Craving
91 ___ gratias
92 Freddy Krueger's street
93 Fatal ending
95 Penn State's lion
97 Paradigm
99 Waterloo, ___, pastry
102 Hallux, e.g.
103 Cat, ___, president
105 Road to Rome
106 Clothes
109 Writer Rand
110 Overcome
113 Spin
114 "The ___ is silence": Shak.
117 Facile
121 Islamic chieftain
122 Place for video games
124 A weather's opposite
125 Adriatic wind
126 Orchestra, ___, lightning rod
128 Caesar, ___, dressing
131 Consumed
132 That, in Toledo
133 "All snug in ___ beds . . ."
134 Columbia paper
135 Words that lead to the altar
136 Between game and match
137 Massachusetts has four
138 Ruhr Valley city

DOWN

1 "Amerika" author
2 Aweigh
3 Getz and Laurel
4 Sycophant
5 Genesis craft
6 Toughen
7 Andrea ___, ill-fated ship
8 Penetrates
9 Dir. of Dallas from Austin
10 "Moonlight ___": Glenn Miller
11 Downfall
12 Ready to scramble
13 Vedic fire god
14 Govt. loan agcy.
15 Talk-show host Mary
16 Plant fiber used in bagging
17 Soho streetcars
18 Medieval merchant guild
24 Manhattan Project physicist
26 Michener epic
30 Sulky
36 Islands of Finland
38 Flower part
40 Mississippi city
42 Breaches
43 Gaelic
44 Restraint
45 "The Third ___" (1949)
46 Water spirits
49 Honey-eating badger
50 Infatuated
51 Impostures
52 Once, once
55 Disney film
56 ___ Twitchit (Beatrix Potter cat)
61 Bothers
63 What you're doing now
65 Jet black
67 Club ___
70 Squeals
73 San Antonio sight
74 His bowlers don't bowl
75 Confirm
76 Ich ___ (Prince of Wales motto)
77 Spanish cooking pot
78 Nebbish
82 Toulouse thought
83 "Bullets Over Broadway" heroine
84 Like Poe's bug
86 Eyelashes
88 Like some sheets
90 Swedish woven rug
94 Washington airport, for short
96 Eau de ___
98 Airheads___
100 Like some library books
101 Stuporous
104 Gave a PG-13 to
107 Distress
108 Expunges
110 Rot
111 Chew the scenery
112 Pecuniary penalties
115 Finley's Dinsmore
116 Vaticinators
118 Falana and Albright
119 Provoked
120 German spa
123 Map features: Abbr.
127 Highs
129 Words of understanding
130 SST heading

50

WHO PLAYED . . .   by Nancy Nicholson Joline
Film buffs sharpen your pencils.

ACROSS

1 Expunged
6 Betel palms
12 Universe
18 Sister of Calliope
19 Actress Helena ___ Carter
20 Journalist Fallaci
21 . . . Salieri in "Amadeus"?
25 Mother Carey's chicken
26 Brian Boru's land
27 Kind of column
28 Bush or Clinton, e.g.
30 Shah Jahan's tomb site
31 Dir. of Venice from Florence
32 Greek T
33 Transparency of animation
35 El ___ (Cher's birthplace)
37 Former Pacific def. gp.
39 . . . Ronny the baker in "Moonstruck"?
43 La preceder
46 Bar
47 Protected African animal
48 Airplane-wing part
49 Crooked
51 "The other ___, demiparadise": Shak.
53 Mine hauling device
56 "___ It a Pity": Gershwin
58 Eulenspiegel of legend
59 . . . the mother in "E.T."?
62 Niçoise, e.g.
64 Falaise friend
67 Symbol of strength
68 Sailor's time units
70 Blair and Hunt
72 Super Bowl VII winners
75 Saint Philip ___
77 "I came, ___ . . ."
79 What i.e. stands for
80 "Dover Beach" poet
82 Sight, for one

84 Leo "The ___" Durocher
86 Juan Carlos I, e.g.
87 "An ___ life for me"
89 . . . Fredo in "The Godfather"?
93 Long
94 Like some Spanish wines
96 Scintilla
97 Vellications
99 Shade of blue
101 Fasten
103 Rome's ___ Veneto
105 ___ Khan
108 According to
109 . . . Holly in "Hannah and Her Sisters"?
113 Chopin and Rubinstein, e.g.
114 Result in
116 Doughboys
117 Neighbor of Ukr.
119 Harris and Wynn
120 Near East port
122 Sniggler's catch
123 Realm
126 City won by Crusaders: 1191
127 Ours, to Orlando
129 . . . Maerose in "Prizzi's Honor"?
133 Ethically neutral
134 Ton of money
135 Silly ones
136 Beliefs
137 Some are frozen
138 Styx locale

DOWN

1 Support
2 They're white in winter
3 Nobelist, e.g.
4 Peut-___ (perhaps)
5 Palme ___ (Cannes award)
6 Arabs' outer garments
7 Rifles
8 Tenor Caruso

9 Oratory
10 Sound of surprise
11 Kilt size
12 Struggling
13 100th part of a krone
14 Indian lute
15 . . . Lois Lane in "Superman"?
16 Individualist
17 Lima living room
22 ___ Khan
23 "Heart of Gold" singer
24 Malls, to teens
29 Ascertains
32 Pith helmet
34 ___ Cruces
36 Congou, e. g.
38 Martin of tennis
40 Jet-engine parts
41 Twist
42 Pitches
44 "___ Me": 1954 song
45 Leatherworker's tool
50 Endure

52 Classic opener
54 White elephant, e.g.
55 Oda ___ Brown (Whoopi in "Ghost")
57 Chess champ Mikhail
60 Halfhearted
61 Grisham bestseller, with "The"
63 Year in the reign of Claudius I
64 Dior follower
65 Wonder
66 . . . the Scots runner in "Chariots of Fire"?
69 Deli items
71 Porcine abode
73 Kind of choral work
74 U.N. agcy.
76 Meet again
78 Guru, for short
81 E.R. figures
83 Na Na lead-in
85 Tap
88 Bumpers' bailiwick
90 Shoreline feature

91 Talks in a babyish way
92 Repeat
93 Egyptian cobra
95 Kind of oil
98 Chose
100 Author LeShan
102 Long John Silver had one
104 Upper heart chambers
106 House of Lancaster symbol
107 Early ascetics
110 Paradigms
111 Dilates
112 Wagnerian heroine
115 ___ nous
118 New Eng. college
120 Premed subj.
121 Feature of St. Peter's
124 Jazzman Hinton
125 One-dollar bills
126 Perplexed
128 Squeal
130 Timberwolves' org.
131 Au ___, menu note
132 Yuck!

51 BASEBALL BEAUS by Jim Page
Expect to go into extra innings with this challenger.

ACROSS

1 Scraps
5 Writer St. Johns
10 Noise
16 Sea bird
18 Additional name
20 Hook-shaped
21 Apparel
22 Stuck on an ex-Twin?
24 Employees' lounge
26 Ethyl finish
27 Wool: Comb. form
28 Tim Conway character
29 Simpleton
31 Stuck on an ex-Yankee?
36 Puts away feed
38 Fed. drugbusters
40 Palindromic Indian
41 That girl
42 Stem joint
43 Virtuoso's asset
44 Montana and Morgan
45 ___ contendere
46 Toward the stern
49 End of a French toast
51 It may be bitter
52 Proserpina's mother
53 Moslem prayer
54 Gumshoes
55 Palm Beach-to-Miami dir.
56 Tree surgeons, often
57 Shutout
59 Cow genus
60 Soldier of fortune
61 Guarantor
62 Single-handed
64 Anti
68 Dreaded disease
69 Thumbs down
70 Have ___ for (dislike)
72 Social levels
75 Bakker's former org.
76 River of Greece
77 "___ eyes close in slumber": Brooke
78 Hurts
79 Heir homophone
80 First counters
81 Sublet
82 Felt bad about
83 Arthurian lady
84 Spring dance?
85 Munch on
87 Labor ender
88 Kingston Trio hit
89 Loan fig.
90 Antiseptics
94 Stuck on an ex-Red?
99 Pop
101 Rikki-Tikki-___
102 Charlie's wife
103 Grave letters
105 Sinatra was one
107 Stuck on an ex-Dodger?
112 On land
113 Racket string
114 Poseidon and Triton
115 Lost a spare tire
116 Bristly
117 Car of the '20s
118 Howard and Maris

DOWN

1 American gymnast
2 Perfumes
3 Stuck on an ex-Blue Jay?
4 Feudal slave
5 Some
6 Hawaii's first governor
7 Write a final draft
8 Pier
9 "Wheel of Fortune" buy
10 Mexican cowboys
11 Vampire
12 "___ for the Misbegotten"
13 Damage
14 Noun suffix
15 Claret-colored
16 ___ deux
17 Slanted
18 Sacked out
19 Stuck on an ex-Twin?
23 Cleared
25 Shallow-water echinoderms
30 "A Drinking Song" poet
32 "___ in the place, except . . ."
33 Minor duty
34 Conger catcher
35 Scum
37 Raffles
39 Backward era?
44 Stuck on an ex-Red Sox player
45 Stuck on an ex-Dodger
46 "___ sang love's old . . ."
47 Highway, in Hamburg
48 MacGraw et al.
50 "Happy Warrior's" monogram
52 Commuted together
55 Villain from Krypton
56 Medieval clan
58 Couples
59 Kite type
60 Giovanni Cimabue, for one
63 Abner's adjective
65 Hacienda hall
66 Old French coins
67 ROK's first president
71 NASDAQ letters
72 Dominican Indian
73 Shrill
74 "Hot Shots!" star
75 Hecuba's husband
76 Little Boy or Fat Man
79 Catch in a sting
80 Gotcha!
83 Arise
86 Oven mitt, e.g.
91 Sioux Santee
92 Father of Tiresias
93 Begot
95 Adventure film of 1995
96 Magic word
97 Lake Indians
98 Flagstad and Sills
100 Energy units
104 Leaf
106 Part of SEATO
107 Chemist's deg.
108 "Diff'rent Strokes" actress
109 Ma Bell, for short
110 Rum Tum Tugger's auth.
111 Poisonous prefix

ACROSS

1 Where to get E-mail
4 Short distance
8 Pack down
12 Astound
17 Annealing oven
19 Wake Island, e.g.
20 Sponge spicule
21 Improve a road
22 Buck chaser
23 Keats poem
24 Golden Valley loc.
25 Mountain pools
26 Who was Othello?
30 Diamonds in the rough
31 Wellington's alma mater
32 Cather's "One of ___"
33 Gilbert in "Roseanne"
34 Anita of jazz
35 Shells
36 Rapping Dr.
39 Extreme orbital point
42 Kitty
43 "Henry and June" role
44 Guitarist Clapton
45 And who was that girl?
51 Put ___ a nutshell
52 Standoffish
53 It may have a tongue
54 Agnes deMille ballet
55 Columbus Day mo.
56 Chi follower
57 Nut
58 Impresario Hurok
59 You mean that mad old woman?
68 Tilling tool
69 Passing marks
70 Ages and ages
71 Plaines
72 Pittsburgh product
75 Switzerland's longest river
76 Thorne Smith's Topper
79 Full fathom five down
80 Where does that guy come in?
84 Designer Jacobsen
85 Ump's cry
86 Lined up
87 Skunk relative
88 Farrow in "The Great Gatsby"
89 Friend in need
90 Bismarck or Kemperer
91 Poverty
93 Fit of temper
94 Disgorge
95 Eternal
99 Heavens, what happened?
104 Novelist Lesage
105 Portent
106 Root or Yale
107 Iris locale
108 Dither
109 "Step ___!"
110 Poly trailer
111 Zenith
112 Revoke a legacy
113 Director De Laurentiis
114 Villain's grimace
115 The limit, sometimes

DOWN

1 Periods of ennui
2 Kentucky college
3 Demonstrated
4 ". . . lion than to ___ hare": Shak.
5 Czech president Masaryk
6 Part of QE2
7 Went into sudden death
8 Hoyden
9 Hypothetical particle
10 Carte
11 Marcel Marceau's forte
12 Maestro Toscanini
13 Boardinghouse offerings
14 Abruzzi bell town
15 Billy in "Sniper"
16 Formerly, formerly
18 Yield, for one
19 Big Dipper star
27 Guns N' Roses guitarist
28 In any way
29 Delhi's river
34 "___ that Shakespearian Rag": Eliot
35 "Tennis, ___?"
36 Stowe title
37 Ordination, e.g.
38 Pining oread
39 Señor's farewell
40 Jeans sew-on
41 Plaza accommodation
42 Play-for-pay person
44 Levi's "Christ Stopped at ___"
46 Cannes cup
47 Lamb's pseudonym
48 "Before thee like ___": Shak.
49 Arabian boat
50 Warble
56 Philadelphia suburb
57 Bandleader Brown
58 Pick up a pebble
60 ___ it's at
61 Batty, in Bath
62 Man of the hour
63 Great Barrier ___
64 Deejay's record
65 Old enough to know better
66 Lamp occupant
67 Werner in "Ship of Fools"
72 Ersatz
73 Garr of "Mr. Mom"
74 Sicilian spouter
75 Maturation
76 Handspring
77 Novel of the South Seas
78 Suture
79 Pay off old debts
81 Borne on the wind
82 Gave Bo a ten
83 Edged
89 47 Down, e.g.
90 ___ suggestion (listening)
91 Shrivel
92 Liaison
93 Grab
94 Knitter's coil
95 Banal
96 Chalet features
97 London broil
98 Tremulous
99 Pro ___
100 Having a nasty smell
101 Complexity
102 Potent beginning
103 Otherwise

53 HALOES AND HORNS by Brad Wilber
Original clues highlight this careful construction.

ACROSS

1 Miscue
5 Dian Fossey subjects
9 "Alexandria Quartet" novel
13 Vengeful Olympian
17 Gounod contemporary
18 Berserk
20 Name in Louisiana politics
21 Ned with a Pulitzer
22 Poet Khayyam
23 Olfactory stimulus
24 Proceedings
25 Suspect's need
26 Cagney classic
30 It rolls in Reno
31 Base stealer Brock
32 Senatorial stance
33 Martino et al.
34 Reacted to a pun
38 Loses a lap
39 Typist's stat
41 Sicilian smoker
42 Revenue
43 Guido's pinnacle
45 Imported cheeses
50 Smeltery dross
51 Pasta selection
53 "Ditto!"
54 Downsize
55 Sourpuss' expression
56 Make eyes at
57 Convertiplane
58 Jubilant
60 Jeff of "The Lawnmower Man"
62 French dog
64 Gala
65 "Turandot" basso
66 Activist Alinsky
67 Early Hanks vehicle
70 Opportunity for discussion
71 Checker move
75 With 77 Down, stability
76 Piner's word
77 Wide-mouthed pitcher
78 Wised up
79 Listing
81 Texan whirlwind
84 Bell-curve figure
85 "Romola" heroine
86 James Herriot, e.g.
87 Straw in the wind
88 Canal craft
89 Wire-service inits.
91 Music critic Downes
92 Mooring line
94 Muslim honorific
97 Tenet
99 Hextall of hockey
100 Meditation syllables
101 Impetuosity
110 Beman of the PGA
111 Aspersion
112 Nightingale, for one
113 Cindy Brady's problem
115 Ruhr hub
116 Jabot material
117 Cortege
118 IOU
119 Soaks flax
120 February figure
121 "Life With Father" star
122 Vicinage

DOWN

1 Mel's Diner redhead
2 Solitary Tibetan
3 ___ Bator
4 Vilas rival
5 Charlotte ___ (Virgin Islands capital)
6 Diagrammed a sentence
7 Sufficient, to Shadwell
8 ___ Valley, CA
9 Botanical spikelet
10 Fixed points
11 Diving judge's concern
12 Variegated pottery
13 Toledo greeting
14 Jong or Morini
15 Revolting one?
16 Fishy
19 Slinky
21 Luftwaffe opponent
27 Ferber or Purviance
28 Aaron Spelling series
29 Jabber
34 Canadian peninsula
35 Lay back
36 Hokkaido seaport
37 World's highest cascade
38 Circumspect
40 Hebrew letter
42 Bolt attachment
43 Keen
44 Trumpet-shaped flower
46 Cliff Richard hit of 1976
47 "___ Troll": Heine
48 Anchor
49 Auctioneer's exclamation
51 Super
52 Unimpressive
55 It has its problems
59 French pronoun
60 Blue-ribbon
61 ___ Darya River
62 Max of boxing
63 Country lane hazard
65 Raise a glass to
66 Poet Silverstein
67 Three-handed card game
68 "Honest to ___!"
69 Mementos for a haole
70 Creosote buildup spot
71 Doppelganger
72 Motionless
73 Phase
74 Facial astringent
76 Recommended
77 See 75 across
80 Greek cross
82 Mulligrubs
83 Lofty
88 "Bei Mir ___ du Schoen"
90 "Mr. ___ Passes By": Milne
91 Holds forth
92 "Happy Days" role
93 City on the Somme
94 Herpetophobe's horror
95 Nene and brant
96 Halt, to salts
98 Shiny balloon polyester
102 Couturiere de la Fressange
103 NFL Hall-of-Famer Ford
104 "Scavenger Hunt" star
105 Mystique
106 Cablecar
107 Forearm
108 A-line pioneer
109 Borgia in-law
114 Shell-game item

ACROSS

1 Busted to PFC
8 Museum piece
13 Field's partner
19 Fatty
20 Charm
22 French tax
23 Birthday request, perhaps
25 Testator's subject
26 Heady brew
27 Blemish
28 They're often given for free
30 Trounced
33 Roomy car
35 Cicero's garment
36 Previous to
37 Ripping
39 Indian friend
41 Word on a door
43 Bridal commitment
44 Bribe
46 Advise
47 Kind of boxer
51 Enticed
54 Nanny's vehicle
56 Below the pecs
58 Broadcast
59 Pinniped places
61 Like skinny-dippers
63 Wholly
64 Orgy cry
65 Horse and wagon
67 Instant photography inventor
69 Resistance unit
70 Dragonfly
75 Danseur's event
76 Apollo's mom
77 Nothing, in Castile
78 River to the Gulf of Finland
79 Songlike
81 City on the Oka
83 Being the chairperson
88 Aquarium attraction
89 High dudgeon
90 No longer on shore
91 He puts the punch in punch
92 Squinted toward
94 Ptolemy's sacred bull
97 Shade tree
99 Gardner biography
100 Criminal
101 Altar slab
103 Actress Jens et al.
106 Teacher's deg.
109 Claudel's "Five Great ___"
111 Forbidding
113 Old German coins
114 212 and 716
117 Within: Comb. form
118 Jackie's second
119 Kind of card
120 Certain errand boys
126 Yellowish-red dye
127 Tawdry
128 Antiseptic solutions
129 Abate
130 Prophets
131 Zagreb locale

DOWN

1 Pappy
2 Dutch city
3 DII x II
4 Sedative
5 "Transfiguration" playwright
6 Early ascetic Palestinians
7 ___ Leppard
8 Act on new evidence
9 Embryonic germ layer
10 An acid salt
11 "Baby ___ Want You": Bread
12 Rum mixer
13 "On the Waterfront" star
14 Warner Bros. hellraiser
15 Poet Dove
16 Make jubilant
17 Modify
18 Reagan cabineteer
21 Observe the Sabbath
24 Alan Ladd film
29 Mausoleums
30 Kettle handles
31 Clothe
32 Greek marketplace
34 Affirmative gesture
38 Most inane
40 Alligator ___ (avocado)
42 Irritated state
45 Historic starter
48 Talk foolishly
49 Forgetfulness
50 Ancient Dead Sea region
52 Ht.
53 Adverse critic
55 Film pooch
57 Neth. neighbor
60 Loggers' sport
61 Hackneyed
62 Surrounded by
63 Arrow poisons
66 Enniskillen river
68 Toughens
70 Taunting one
71 Type size
72 Access
73 Fiber ends
74 Art style of the '20s
75 Insulation strip
80 French department
82 Pack of paper
84 Arikara
85 Veni, to a Latin student
86 "___ Love a Stranger" (1958)
87 Anaheim Stadium surface
89 Ran in neutral
90 Yes man
93 Phantom
95 Foot
96 Acute
98 Toro's foe
102 USSR cooperatives
104 U.S.–Mexican border city
105 "Twelfth Night" noblewoman
106 Of the Vatican
107 Hive loafer
108 Mexican elevations
110 Autumn mo.
112 Bergen loc.
115 Court figs.
116 Hindustani Messrs.
121 Hero ending
122 Thus
123 Savings amt.
124 Hawaiian decoration
125 Retirees' paymaster

ACROSS

1 "Delphine" novelist
6 Superboy's girlfriend
10 Manhandle
13 On the road
17 Of a blood vessel
19 Over
20 Further
21 First name in spydom
22 HIGH
25 Make espresso
26 Marine paintings
27 Some are hooked
28 Streisand's "___ in Love"
29 Part of O.H.M.S.
30 Rights org.
31 Tax specialist
33 Poetic monogram
34 Joined securely
39 HIGH
42 Mountains of the Kirghiz
43 In ecstasy
45 Origin
46 Queen of Spain
48 Road Runner's sound
50 Final word of "Ulysses"
51 "OED" listings
55 HIGH
60 Young Guthrie
61 Takes care of
62 Syn. for facing
63 Pipe
64 Horned snake
66 HIGH
72 Krazy ___
73 After photo or turkey
75 Strain ___ gnat
76 Porter and Ness
78 Travel
79 HIGH
86 Crafts' partner
87 ___ Plaines
88 Nonpareil
89 Loving one
90 Ukranian seaport
93 Letters on a Stealth
95 Star of "Assault on a Queen"
96 HIGH

101 Dew, e.g.
104 Filch
105 Abbr. in a real estate ad
106 Building wings
107 Mouth: Comb. form
108 Exhausted
110 Gdansk native
111 Opposing successfully
117 Liz's famous role
118 HIGH
121 For fear that
122 Retired
123 Spree
124 Suriname locale
125 "¿Como ___?"
126 ___ culpa
127 Angered
128 "I know not why I am ___": Shak.

DOWN

1 Declines in value
2 Divided or disrupted
3 Territory
4 Athenian letters
5 Chinese nut
6 Do dockwork
7 Actor Roscoe
8 Fall mo.
9 Glimpse
10 Bursts
11 "We ___ the World"
12 Attach firmly
13 Early Christian pulpit
14 Enthusiasm
15 Sergeant's command
16 Gaped
18 Sculptor Oldenburg
20 Aspen bumps
23 Belgian town
24 Subside

28 Female WW2 fighter
30 Miller's "___ the Fall"
31 Oil bottle
32 Intrinsically
34 Friable earth
35 Butterine
36 Leader
37 Trace
38 Lienee, e.g.
40 Fluctuate
41 Moth repellent wood
44 Recent: Comb. form
47 "Stop being ___!"
49 In proportion
52 Composer of "Socrate"
53 Type of market
54 Fashion
56 Elastic wood
57 RR stop

58 PC graphic image type
59 Speed meas.
63 Light-colored
64 Nora's pooch
65 Restaurateur Toots
67 Average
68 Indian of the Platte
69 Checked the thermometer again
70 Pau pronoun
71 Weeks per annum
74 Director Welles
77 Turn round and round
79 Music hall
80 Waistcoats
81 He, to Sophia
82 Ponchielli's "Dance of the ___"
83 Manny has two
84 Tree home
85 Pitcher Dressendorfer

91 "Rats!"
92 Ancient
94 Scowl
96 Infallible utterance
97 "La Cage aux ___"
98 Most talented
99 Paris publication
100 Warns
102 Chimp's cousin
103 Permeable by water
109 Whit
110 Excuse
111 God in a chariot
112 Odium
113 Type of combo
114 "___ corny as Kansas . . ."
115 Zola protagonist
116 Pleased
118 Woolen cap
119 Man on a five
120 Very

56 BARHOPPING by Fred Piscop
Fred got this idea while visiting Hershey, PA.

ACROSS

1 Dillon and LeBlanc
6 Hullabaloo
10 Gadget
16 Sleepwear
19 Write off: Abbr.
20 Ebert's thumbs-up
21 Request formally
22 Ending for fin
23 SNICKERS
26 Shih ___
27 Rock's ___ Brothers
28 Dusseldorf duck
29 Sight from Le Havre
30 Complexity
31 Perpetually
33 Greasy residues
36 Short-billed rail
38 CHUNKY
45 Fleur-de-___
46 Thurman in "Pulp Fiction"
47 Speaker who batted .344
48 Platitudinous
49 ___' acte
51 Lee or Cass
54 Troop's camp
57 Peruvian of yore
58 Stag partygoers
60 MILKY WAY
63 Brokers
65 Tallow source
66 Grid great Dickerson
67 Suitor's request
68 JFK abbr.
70 Brittany city
73 Stroller rider
74 Dog with webbed feet
77 Florentine river
79 Board's partner
81 Marinara ingredient
83 MARS
88 Dragster's fuel
89 "Topaz" author
91 "La ___ Vita" (1960)
92 Tossed in a chip
94 "Out of Mulberry Street" author
95 Singer Staples
97 The Allman Brothers' "___ Peach"
99 Long-tailed monkey
100 Wacko
101 MOUNDS
108 Windows 95 symbol
109 Glacial spur
110 Certain
111 Leon in "Peyton Place"
114 MCPO's org.
116 Pusher's pursuer
118 Experienced
122 Shake
123 CRUNCH
127 Wrath
128 10th-century Pope
129 Villa d'
130 Masquerade
131 Singer McLean
132 Think
133 Like batik
134 Skip over

DOWN

1 Hazel, for one
2 Shells, but not ziti
3 "___ the mornin'!"
4 "Jeopardy" host
5 Make an exerted effort
6 An Ember Day: Abbr.
7 "Lady Beware" star
8 Exact satisfaction
9 Suppressed
10 "The Crying Game" hairdresser
11 "Swinging ___ Star"
12 Egg
13 Compendium
14 Beating
15 Marion's "___ Grieux"
16 Pocketed bread
17 Utah cagers
18 Marshy pool
24 Prepares to drive
25 Ideology
30 Mold
32 "___ Is Bleeding" (1994)
34 Susman of tennis
35 Vexations
37 Dirt-road feature
38 Article length
39 Carpet fibers
40 Wise man
41 Grammarian's concern
42 Tim
43 And so forth
44 "Bad Behavior" star
45 Curtis of aviation
50 Cartoon chihuahua
52 Lawn pest
53 River of Flanders
55 ___ and parcel
56 "Silas Marner" author
59 Prepare vegetables
61 "In ___": Nirvana album
62 Literary Bell
64 Valuable violin
69 ___ Domini
71 Soft seat
72 Podunk, for one
74 Hispanic
75 Skylit court
76 Do a PR job
78 Lascivious looker
80 Island off China
82 It docked with Atlantis
83 Cleave
84 Husband of Isis
85 Florida city
86 Get in the way of
87 Brings up
89 John L. Lewis' org.
90 Metrodome shout
93 Water down
96 Vanderbilt's conference
98 Political battlefield
102 Put up
103 Get rid of a loafer
104 Phonied up
105 Hugh Latimer's crime
106 Lorraine locale
107 Act the middleman
111 Like the Kalahari
112 "Still Life with Coffee" painter
113 Novelist Phillpotts
115 "Walk This World" singer
117 ___ d'Azur
119 Marina Sirtis role
120 Mild oath
121 Flood prevention
123 Peddler in "Oklahoma!"
124 Western NY college
125 Cause for a shootout
126 Greenspan's org.

57 HIGHLY ILLUMINATING   by Frances Hansen
A brilliant work from a star cruciverbalist.

ACROSS

1 Spiny-finned fish
5 Cut corners
10 Twice CDLII
14 Grants
19 Spooky canal?
20 Aesop's postscript
21 Loathe
22 Christening tap
23 First divine proclamation
26 "My Life in Court" author
27 Like mortarboards
28 Revolutionary hero Silas
29 Gave a Bronx cheer
30 FDR's dog
31 Capital of Guam
32 Wild
33 ___-pants (know-it-all)
36 Ridge
37 ___ waiting (royal attendants)
39 Devil's domain
40 Stanley Kubrick film
42 Pen point
44 Mahler's "Das Lied von der ___"
45 Journalist Huntley
46 ___ side (awry)
48 Brownies' org.
49 TV alien
50 Holden-Baxter film
54 Nasser's successor
56 Radiation
58 Out of sorts
59 Sloping
60 Concorde wing
61 Pilfered
62 Bring up
63 Condemned
65 Concerning
66 Handle
69 Town on the Allegheny
70 Kidder film, with "The"
73 Classic prefix
74 Fleur-de-___
75 Old enough to know better
77 Ambiance
78 Maidenhair, for one
79 MD time
80 Jennifer Beals film
84 Perlman's aid
85 Poe poem
88 Buenos ___
89 Liverpool river
90 Greek cheeses
91 Potts of "Designing Women"
92 ___ Sound, FL
93 Ticket
95 "___ a Man": Willingham novel
96 Start of a Hemingway title
100 Guarneri's teacher
101 "But when a god-given ___": Pindar
103 Veronica in "Sessions"
104 Aleutian air base
105 Soissons river
106 "Green Mansions" heroine
107 Author Hite
108 Writer Koontz
109 Laud
110 "Doggone!"

DOWN

1 Big gulp of liquor
2 District
3 Makes a lap
4 Liberates
5 Reeking
6 Kwangju locale
7 Teed off
8 "Queen ___": Shelley
9 Future frat brothers
10 Tuscany wine
11 ___ cum laude
12 "___ Jury": Spillane
13 Track doc
14 Lie
15 Doolittle and Reed
16 "There is in God some say, a deep but ___": Henry Vaughan
17 Laura Chiesa's sword
18 Chalcedony
24 Preliminary races
25 Rover's restraint
29 Royal rule
31 Mountain ridge
32 Orale
33 Bundle of wheat
34 Mrs. Trump
35 Words from Ovid
36 At the home of
37 Cretan labyrinth builder
38 After Adar
40 Not this
41 Lasso loop
43 Sheet of matted cotton
45 Like crosswords
47 Dead Sea Scrolls preserver
50 Donizetti's "Anna ___"
51 Eight singers
52 Facade
53 "Blue Chips" star
55 Jai ___
57 Director Wertmuller
59 Waft from the kitchen
61 Fits of temper
63 Hawaii's first governor
64 Tilting, asea
65 Poe's godfather
66 Oliver's request
67 Weird
68 "Moonstruck" hero
70 Red: Heraldry
71 Rajah's wife
72 Duchesses' husbands
76 C-sharp, on the piano
78 Proem
81 Saturday night special
82 Alice's cat
83 Bristles
84 Violin's ancestor
86 "___ Skelter": Beatles
87 Prima ballerina
89 Crumb
91 Author Loos
92 "The Pobble who ___ toes . . .": Lear
93 Words from Ebenezer
94 Oriental servant
95 Art Deco designer
96 Song or gab trailer
97 Arabian bigwig
98 Golf's "Champagne Tony"
99 Prelaw exam
101 Michael Jackson album
102 Thumbs down

58 EXPLORING 42 ACROSS by Eileen Lexau
A culinary creation from St. Paul.

ACROSS

1 Idiots
6 Not responsive
10 Busch Gardens site
15 Felt hat
16 Veil material
17 Bellhop's doing
19 Great-grandma's treat
21 Brandy cocktail
23 Arafat's org.
24 Ibis relative
25 Catholic layman
27 Nylons
28 Auto pioneer
30 Be nosy
32 "___ Pretty": Bernstein
33 Region
34 Michelangelo work
36 Carolina rails
38 Writer Serling
39 Gnarl
40 Madden
42 Where we are in this puzzle
44 "In the ___ of life ..."
45 Musical sign
47 Manitoba Indian
48 Partner of mell
49 Lincoln trademark
54 Altitude standard
58 Virginia of tennis
59 Bit
60 Marsh birds
62 Gov. Hogg's daughter
63 Desertlike
64 Eyelashes
66 Bartlett and Cornice
67 "All My ___ Live In Texas"
68 Play about Capote
69 Hartford team
71 ___ Lanka
72 Torn
73 Haydn work
75 Amortization methods
79 Pacific ___ College
80 Icer's tool
81 Word of approval
82 Snap finish
84 "___ and Far Away": Kern
87 Mideast capital
91 Paint thinners, for short
92 Clucking mama
93 Kind of heater
95 Pool member
96 "Blume in Love" drifter
97 Campus squares
99 Bridge coups
101 Arab ruler
102 Jay of baseball
103 George of the Jungle's mate
105 Bread spreads
107 Siouan people
108 "The more the ___"
110 Insincere affection
113 Admirable Mother
114 Pick up the bill
115 Grew
116 Scroungy
117 Chipper
118 ___ Park, CO

DOWN

1 Cereal premium of old
2 Keats opus
3 Tennis shots
4 Steps quickly
5 Early Englishmen
6 Pair
7 Nevada city
8 Out
9 "Be my guest!"
10 Assayed
11 Russian co-op
12 Medical scanner
13 Beg
14 Longhaired felines
15 ___ the blanks
16 "The Bridges at ___"
18 Abandon
20 Shepherd's staff
22 "___ Love": Beatles
23 Orale wearer
26 Long, long time
29 Really hungry
31 Jeans sew-on
35 "The African Queen" screenwriter
37 "Shoo!"
39 Beverly of opera
41 Crystal vision
43 Excited
44 Money
46 Some Prado paintings
48 Ocular activity
49 Goes for a fly
50 Like macadam
51 Hatred
52 Chummy
53 Entertainer Adams
54 Lambchop's friend
55 Spitfire
56 Correct
57 Wears well
61 Escritoire
64 What nervous players do
65 Incendiarism
67 Learned
69 "___ for dinner?"
70 Carols
74 Salmagundi
76 Wagon tongues
77 Caviar clump
78 Opponents
80 Emulates Ozawa
82 Goatfish
83 Like the stegosaurus
84 Meadows
85 Lummox
86 Florida city
88 Takes away
89 Married
90 Matador's adversary
91 Reds or Blues
92 Cheer
94 Come out
97 Mission
98 Sip hot soup
100 Fountain treats
104 Epigone
106 Buttonhole
109 Comparative suffix
111 ___ scallops
112 "A Chorus Line" finale

59 WHERE'S THE BEEF? by Manny Nosowsky
The answer to Manny's title can be found below.

ACROSS

1 Lock up tight
5 Smokey watcher
9 "Amo, ___, I love a lass"
13 Aspire
19 Amy Tan character
20 Guesser's words
21 Besmirch
22 Shawm player
23 Complain, usually
26 Ready to go
27 Traffic tie-ups
28 "___ Marianne": Osmond hit
29 Matriculate
31 Give the slip
34 Complain loudly
39 Little Caesar
42 Rieger of "Taxi"
43 Cut a curl
44 Idling gear
45 Complain
48 Fathomless
50 Gossip
51 "Charles in Charge" star
52 Hampton ___
54 Charlie McCarthy's friend
57 Joan of Arc's god
58 ___ of (amazed by)
60 Make a mess of
61 Sag some
63 Conversation hesitations
64 NFL team, for short
66 Metric measure of volume
69 "I got ___ in Kalamazoo . . ."
71 Complains
78 Romanov ruler
79 Yammered
80 ___ rima (abababcc)
81 Taxi
84 Civil rights leader Medgar
87 Straw beehive
89 Key
90 Marie Saint et al.
92 Keep an ___ (watch)
94 Formal attire
96 Caen's river
97 March of ___
99 Calais cop
101 Complain
103 Balkan state
106 Prefix for phobia
108 Franklin stove fuel
109 AA candidate
110 Complain
112 Opera hero, as a rule
114 Aquatic nymph
115 Swift and Snyder
117 "Star Trek" weapon
121 T-bone and sirloin
124 Complain
128 Stops dreaming
129 Actress Skye
130 Witch's end in a tale
131 Where Yazd is
132 Texas town of song
133 Have-not's condition
134 Knoxville st.
135 Great ___

DOWN

1 Unhappy expressions
2 UAE neighbor
3 Kilauea outflow
4 Not here
5 Like the Foreign Service
6 Bikini part
7 ME time
8 Campus marchers
9 Be amazing
10 Canadian constabulary
11 First follower
12 Macbeth murdered it
13 Raspy
14 Disgrace
15 Annoyed the EPA
16 Where Witt whirls
17 Contemporary of e.e.c.
18 He had 1,860 RBIs
24 Mitigate
25 Devilkins
30 N Thailand province
32 Indoor design
33 Tire out
35 Topple
36 Palmer, to pals
37 Fire fighter?
38 Actor Brandauer
39 Leaving with the tide
40 Not a nice guy
41 Flexible
46 At the nadir
47 Mrs. Woodrow Wilson
49 Part of RPM
53 Act the villain
55 Gray-sorrel
56 Out of sight
59 Irregular
62 Page of music
65 Polished in manner
67 Elvis' long-time label
68 ___ Stavro Blofeld
70 Plenty
72 It beats a deuce
73 Mammy or Pappy
74 Not precise
75 "I Am the ___": Beatles
76 Still
77 "Have you heard the ___?"
81 Moth-repellant wood
82 St. Theresa's town
83 Thumper's friend
85 Ring official
86 ___ plexus
88 Tea type
91 Oceanic ophidian
93 Skin-patch drug
95 "Dead Man Walking" star
98 Went quietly
100 Sang like Bing
102 With "oe," a state song
104 Yea
105 Revelation word
107 "All ___": 1931 song
111 Newman or Hubble
113 Berserk
116 Piggy-bank feature
118 Asmodeus' love
119 Israel's Abba
120 Sandberg of baseball
121 "Erie Canal" mule
122 United rival
123 Musical talent
125 Attack the weeds
126 "___ Gotta Be Me"
127 Perception

ENDANGERED SPECIES by Rand H. Burns
We hope these thematic entries don't join the dodo and moa.

ACROSS

1 Pretentious
5 Dizzy Gillespie's forte
10 Conflagrant
15 Ready for surgery
19 Young Saarinen
20 Winged
21 Pinched
22 Kent's coworker
23 Rare African ungulate
25 Rare Chinese mammal
27 Kin to "ouch!"
28 M1 tank, e.g.
29 French military academy
31 Gossip
32 Croaker
35 Hawthorne's home
37 Australian willow
41 Clueless
42 Regarding
44 Deserved
46 Actress Maryam d'___
47 Oxide of element number 65
49 1994 Costner role
51 Offhand
53 Rare mountain-dwelling cat
57 Student at 29 Across
58 Stand out
62 Pataki's predecessor
63 Lowly
64 Armor-plated, as armadillos
66 Seism
68 Fermented drink
71 Captain of the Pequod
72 High-IQ group
75 Garfield's wail: Var.
76 Nine-to-fiver's acronym
77 Wistful thinking
78 Musical triplets
80 Short poem
82 Beatles song
84 Precip ending
86 Pollen bearers
87 Jidda resident
89 Rare omnivore of Alaska
92 Abnormally introverted
94 Spud bud remover
95 Hard-pressed
100 Allen of 1776
101 Champ
104 Catcher's putdown?
106 Goldberg's Palooza
107 Lie
109 Maine and Ohio, to Gauls
111 Prosodic
113 Titan matriarch
115 Compounds
117 IBM competitor
118 Wherein all learn to soldier: Abbr.
119 Rare aquatic mammal
123 Rare African primate
126 Cacao, e.g.
127 Lofty habitation
128 Alaskan peninsula
129 Israeli machine guns
130 Harness
131 Activity ctrs.
132 Less ditsy
133 Prong

DOWN

1 Stunt pilot
2 Put up elsewhere
3 Flirt
4 Thither and ___
5 Rare Asian ruminant
6 Ailavator
7 Preclude
8 Some early Iowans
9 Gadflies
10 Diamond footwear
11 More sporting
12 Pig ___ poke
13 Marmalade ingredient
14 Sweet-talks
15 Greek philosopher
16 Managed
17 Result
18 Green shade
24 Simple Simon
26 Cineaste
30 Bivouac
33 Workshop
34 Waxed
36 Small unit of pressure
38 Rare piscator of North America
39 Fit
40 Country singer Axton
43 Suffix with ether
45 Modicum
48 Time between ticks
50 VCR button
52 Rhine tributary
54 Mink relative
55 "Invictus," e.g.
56 Bishop's-weed, to a taxonomist
58 Not real
59 Mies van der ___
60 Rare anthropod of the Sunda Islands
61 Trigonal sail
63 Rare Andean ungulate
65 Ring
67 Promiscuous
69 Encumbrance
70 Young newts
73 Successor to Ramses I
74 The gamut
76 President pro ___
78 Baseball's Speaker
79 Crêpe ___
81 Mend
83 Amin
85 Duplicitous
87 Levantine ketch
88 Subtle emanation
89 Scat!
90 Kind of man
91 Homburg part
93 High water channel
96 Liston's dethroner
97 Hot tub
98 Where Monty turned back Rommel
99 Bluish cat
102 Livorno's locale
103 Apparel for Benazir Bhutto
105 Botanical buds
108 Jibe
110 Football stats
112 Victrola mfr.
114 Throaty notice
116 Queens stadium
119 Hampshire's home
120 Golf instructor
121 Musophobiac's cry
122 Trajectory
124 Resting place
125 Eccentric

DADDY DEAREST   by Fran and Lou Sabin
Here's a perfect puzzle to solve on Father's Day.

ACROSS

1 Prayer wheel user
5 Dancer Moiseyev
9 Lamentation
13 Beef
18 Napoleon was one
20 Director Clair
21 Cradle call
22 Aqua ___
23 Jack's dad
25 In a short time
26 "The Country Girl" dramatist
27 Feeling guilt
28 Jamie's dad
30 Poet's monogram
31 Rod's companion
32 She loved Aeneas
33 Chin attachment
34 Shari's dad
38 St. Louis gridder
41 Candy nuts
44 Bundy and Unser
45 Scale syllables
46 Audition topic
47 ___ garde
48 Yothers of "Family Ties"
50 Captain of ill repute
52 Reed under Mehta
53 Encircle
54 Marlo's dad
57 Lady's escort
58 Cockney inferno
59 Stones
60 Actress Brejchova
61 Habituates
63 Abuse
65 Chaney in "The Miracle Man"
66 Map line
68 Some pants have them
70 Mobile one
72 Copenhagen or Champion
73 Pitcher, metaphorically
76 Sam Lane's daughter
77 Charlie's dad
80 VIII x LXIX
81 Designer Klein
82 "Welcome" bearers
83 Writes "wierd"
84 "They ___ Believe Me": Kern
85 Exigency

86 Holm
87 Half a Kikuyu terrorist org.
88 Desert delusion
89 Famed NHL defenseman
90 Stephanie's dad
95 Manner
96 Evasive
97 "Critique of Pure Reason" author
98 "Leave It to Beaver" actor
101 Michael's dad
106 Cultural belief: Var.
108 "Moonstruck" song
109 Work hard
110 Bridget's dad
112 Stanford Olsen, e.g.
113 Ligurian Sea feeder
114 Chinese gelatin
115 Admiral's command
116 Scholar's collars
117 Miami five
118 Catapult
119 Good Friday's time

DOWN

1 Competed in Calaveras County
2 Sedan shafts
3 Tigger's creator
4 Jai follower
5 Press agent?
6 With affection
7 Toddler's age
8 In medias ___
9 Christopher Plummer's daughter
10 They go with milk and honey
11 Plump god
12 Fit to stand trial
13 Graze
14 Give a new hue to

15 "The Morning Watch" novelist
16 Gold-medalist skater
17 Crosby, Stills & ___
19 Contestant
24 Boos
28 Feels poorly
29 Prohibition opponents
32 Filibuster
34 Bridge unit
35 Premarital posting
36 Hals or Bosch
37 Zip
38 Alan's dad
39 Detached
40 Fulfills
41 Errand boy
42 Like Mr. Scratch
43 Rob's dad
46 Vicious elephant
48 Like Shaq
49 Bring together

50 "I Feel For You" singer
51 Tiriac of tennis
54 Form of faith
55 Spinule
56 Temptress
59 Sgt.'s underling
62 Writer Buntline
64 Mitigated
65 Polynesian wear
67 These must be crossed
68 Dallas suburb
69 Individualist
71 Hubbell teammate
72 Carolina allspice, e.g.
74 Senior's wear
75 Grain
78 Mideast leader
79 Run-down
80 Whispered info
84 Female
86 Beautician's creation

87 Wire measures
88 Clementine's dad
90 Downy ducks
91 Mercouri in "Topkapi"
92 Fanatic
93 Japanese dogs
94 Bucket brigade
95 Ohio Ballet home
98 Recipient
99 Marie Osmond's birthplace
100 Virgil Earp's brother
101 Capshaw in "Just Cause"
102 "Since ___ You, Baby": Sonny Jam
103 Kenyan track star
104 Great Salt Lake state
105 Impale
107 Dangle
110 Bit of butter
111 Self-esteem

62 SIDEKICK by Joel D. Lafargue
Joel suggests using the buddy system while solving this.

ACROSS

1 Some are inflated
5 Merrill in "True Colors"
9 Inventor of root beer
14 Arrived
18 Wow!
19 See 86 Down
20 Province in Old Castile
21 Russian range
22 Celebration
23 Freud contemporary
24 Chapter, but no verse
25 It starts in September
26 **Start of an Albert Camus quote**
30 Poodle type
31 Vallone in "A Gunfight"
32 Working man's concern
33 **More of the quote**
42 Arafat's grp.
45 Solo of "Star Wars"
46 Forage plant
47 Génissiat Dam site
48 Glimpse
49 Best and Purviance
51 Cherry feature
53 Tea-time treat
54 Welk's Zimmer
55 Don King's rival
56 **More of the quote**
59 Item on the condiment tray
61 Booty
62 "Midnight Blue" songwriter
63 Louis and James
64 "Vaya Con ___"
66 Madison Ave. product
68 "Return of the Jedi" creature
70 Tamandua tidbit
73 State-run game
76 Comment from a pen pal?
79 Kite relative
83 **Author of quote, in 1957**
87 Weblike tissue
88 "The Remains of the Day" director
89 Squirrel stash
90 Chariot ending
91 "Animal House" wear
92 Rational
93 Delectable dish
94 Unbelievable one
96 TLC dispensers
97 Scrape together
98 **More of the quote**
103 After April in Paris
104 Assist
105 Ab ___ (from the beginning)
106 **End of the quote**
116 None other but
117 Bogey's "Mad Dog" role
118 Ceiling
119 Neill or Coward
121 Search thoroughly
122 Hardship
123 In ___ and drabs
124 Chip's chipmunk pal
125 It's at one end of a choir
126 Hit the hay
127 Sun. talks
128 Old rug style

DOWN

1 Chicken preceder?
2 Spur
3 Frogner Park locale
4 Crude building
5 André Breton's early genre
6 "___ have to do"
7 "Knucksie" of baseball
8 Rooftop item
9 Neither most nor least
10 Novello of silents
11 Anti-crime acronym
12 ___ vital
13 Soup cracker
14 Some are down at the heel
15 "My Name Is ___": Saroyan
16 Drake or gander
17 Pipe joint
19 "Since first I ___ fresh . . .": Shak.
27 Cookout tool
28 Patriots' org.
29 Kitchen scrap
33 "___ a Symphony"
34 Niña's mom
35 Abolish
36 Bark cloth
37 Extra
38 They know the score: Abbr.
39 "___ Killing the Great Chefs of Europe?" (1978)
40 Singer Fargo
41 Tense
42 Salon waves
43 "American Graffiti" star
44 Gives approval
48 Luau fare
50 Surrounded by
52 Win for Tyson
53 Deposit
54 Fragrant alcohol
56 Crane call
57 Tropical snake
58 Hungry kitten, e.g.
60 Ridiculous
65 Narrow waterway
67 Sundial hour
69 Bruce Lee's TV role
70 Absinthe flavoring
71 "Bell, Book and Candle" actress
72 Bluesman Walker
74 Thai weight
75 Layer of concern
77 Compass letters
78 It has a certain ring
80 Pola in pictures
81 Large antelope
82 Cafe cup
84 "Able was I ___ I . . ."
85 Earth goddess
86 With 19 Across, "Mercure" composer
91 Fountain of fame
93 Canceling machines
95 Scrubs the launch
98 Bert Bobbsey's sib
99 Smidgen
100 Puts to use
101 Think the world of
102 "And ___ our tale . . ."
103 It's possible
106 L–Q connection
107 Shady trees
108 Monopoly corner
109 Exhort
110 Blackthorn
111 Maryland athlete
112 Frosty giant
113 Little falsehoods
114 Wyle of "ER"
115 Walter ___ Mare
116 Wood sorrel
120 Journey segment

Q&A   by Tom & Fay Gieschi
The "Q" begins at 3 Down; the "A" at 28 Across.

ACROSS

1 Gambol
5 Ripped
10 "Dancing Queen" group
14 Jezebel's husband
18 Turkish regiment
19 Winglike
20 Yankee Yogi
22 "___ and Get It": Beatles
23 Pierre's mother
24 Greets the day
25 "So Fine" star
26 Silly bloke
27 Type of sauce
28 **Start of the answer**
31 Pres. monogram
32 "O Sole ___"
34 Bar order
35 Byrd's fox terrier
37 Young cod
39 Prompter
41 Photo: Slang
43 Napped
46 Chiffonier
47 Greek letter
49 Salad name
50 ___ day now
51 Requires
53 Artillery box
55 NE Ohio campus
56 Fluids
58 Ambush
60 Frozen
61 Former spy org.
62 Racing shell
63 "Corinne" novelist
65 Nabokov work
66 Consecration vessel
68 Best ending
69 Solecizes
70 Maple genus
71 Row
72 Winter capital of Bihar
74 Turner of history
75 Vice ___
76 Panatela
79 Caviar
80 Appear
82 Baylor site
83 Near East pastry

85 Whale
86 Ravage
88 Kind of metabolism
90 Director Underwood
91 Energy type
93 Sideways
95 Make a script even better
97 Craze
98 Gel
99 French head
100 Glacial ridge
101 St. Petersburg neighbor
103 Ref. bk.
104 Female lobster
105 "The ___ of the Roses" (1989)
107 **Answer: Part III**
114 Shellback
117 Israeli airline
119 Pianist Rubenstein
120 Mrs. Jock Ewing
121 On the mark
122 Nagy of Hungary
123 Guild of yesteryear
124 River of France
125 Legion
126 X and gamma
127 Bikeway
128 Fleer
129 Fleecy females

DOWN

1 Butts
2 TV backdrop
3 **Start of the question**
4 Cherry or apple
5 Indian dress
6 Landed
7 Wear's partner
8 French seasons
9 Wants
10 Over

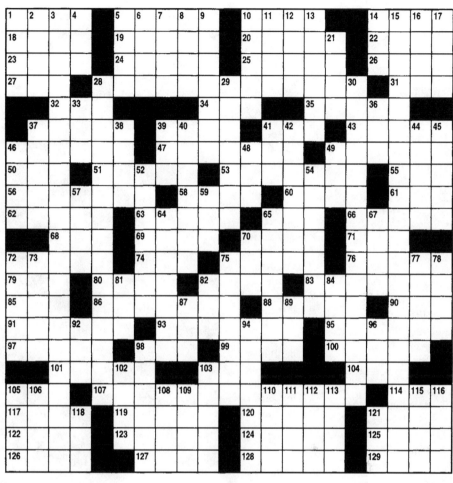

11 Nota ___
12 Remus Fox
13 Numeral type
14 Behave
15 **End of the question**
16 In the thick of
17 ___ noire
21 "Shake ___!" (hurry)
28 **End of the answer**
29 Singsong
30 **Answer: Part II**
33 Rage
36 Corrida cheer
37 Language of Carthage
38 Litigated
39 Tobacco quid
40 Brat
41 Taro product
42 Guts

44 Old hat
45 Word on a quarter
46 Paris proms
48 ___ of luxury
49 Miler Sebastian
52 Dead Sea Scrolls finders
54 Oriental beetles
57 ___ Bator
59 Legal point
64 Run roughshod
65 Wirewalker
67 Sora
70 NRC forerunner
72 Tournament type
73 Trunk in a trunk
75 Parked cars
77 French-I verb
78 Rage
81 Common Market init.
82 Humor

84 Interlaken's river
87 Type of meal
89 Pub order
92 Ballerina Slavenska
94 Rubicundity
96 Make do with
98 Tyrant
102 Egyptian god
103 Winfrey
105 Dam
106 Soprano Gluck
108 Spirit lamp
109 Oxidize
110 Composer Hovhaness
111 Gin berry
112 Demarcation
113 Insulting stare
115 River to The Wash
116 Red and black, e.g.
118 Bandleader Elgart
121 Tea, in Toulon

64 ANIMAL CRACKERS   by Norma Steinberg
Like the song says, "It's all happening at the zoo!"

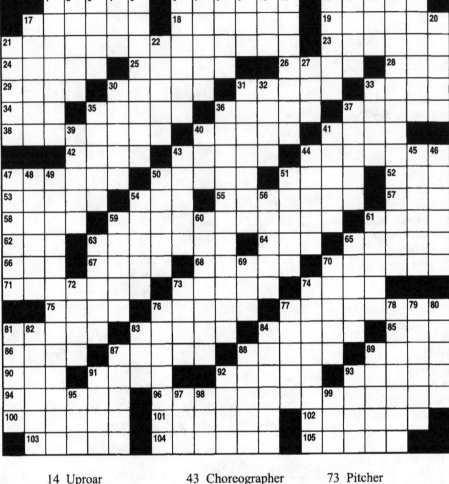

ACROSS

1 Gyrate
6 Buy
12 Pretension
17 Musical Wonder
18 Collegiate cohabitant
19 Eskers
21 Willy, after the movies?
23 Quantity
24 ___ Angels
25 Pantyhose color
26 "No way!"
28 ___ moment's notice
29 Synagogue enclosures
30 Leg parts
31 Bank transactions
33 Glitch
34 Undershirt
35 Steep, as tea
36 Overcharge
37 Positive thinker
38 Dregs
40 Malediction
41 Tulip's beginning
42 March "lion"
43 Rental sign
44 Unblemished
47 Distributes
50 Peachy
51 Bummer!
52 MacGraw in "Players"
53 "Hec Ramsey" star
54 Singer Orbison
55 Eye or nose
57 Nautical diary
58 Part of IRA
59 Privileges of some high-fliers?
61 Peaceful bird
62 Sigma follower
63 Paper-folding art
64 Kanga's child
65 Seagoing vessel
66 Aliens
67 Compassion
68 "For ___ sake!"
70 "Serial Mom" director
71 Diminish
73 Comic Kovacs
74 Bed
75 Israeli dance
76 Göteborg resident
77 Cowboy
81 "The Last Boy ___" (1991)
83 Mating game
84 Hooligans
85 Goof
86 Stretched tight
87 French couple's pronoun
88 Sabulous
89 Pit-stop need
90 Org. that audits
91 Lampblack
92 Nanook's coat
93 Cameroon neighbor
94 Icy
96 Musteline mix-up?
100 Ending
101 Surrey embellishment
102 Aunt Blabby's portrayer
103 Encourage
104 Pouring aid
105 Devoured

DOWN

1 Tracked
2 "The Time Machine" author
3 "Jimmy Crack Corn" singer
4 Former Brazilian capital
5 Sinistra
6 Circa
7 Marine ___
8 Pigeon home
9 Kiwi kin
10 Brooch
11 Adolescent
12 Dicey game
13 Daiquiri ingredient
14 Uproar
15 Reclusive lizard's request?
16 Cognitive
17 Actress North
20 Phase
21 "___ up, Doc?"
22 Indistinct
27 "___ less bell to answer . . ."
30 English guns
31 Rhine siren
32 Evict
33 With respect or admiration
35 Smack
36 Mew mates?
37 Handbag
39 "___ dance, don't make me . . ."
40 Cedar Rapids college
41 Chicago team
43 Choreographer Tharp
44 Outermost planet
45 A cover crop
46 Clemson team
47 Lessened
48 Find
49 Inexpensive overrun dwelling?
50 Drenched
51 Friend of Aramis
54 "Something to Talk About" singer
56 See eye to eye
59 Susan Lucci role
60 Carlotta was one
61 Former coach of 41 Down
63 Victor Visarely's genre
65 Does without
69 Windsor, for one
70 Off the wall
72 Drubbing
73 Pitcher
74 Redford role
76 Plumbing valve
77 Swindle
78 Class action?
79 Beaver State
80 Synthetic fabric
81 Unbending
82 Sissy Spacek film
83 Head exec
84 Bundle
87 "Wanda" director
88 Noncom nickname
89 Moat
91 Granary
92 Keystone State founder
93 Gruff
95 Rib tickler
97 Jay Presson Allen play
98 Pewter component
99 LAX overseer

ACROSS

1 Leveling stick
5 Colonus
9 Became revealed, with 91 Down
13 Alexander of "Seinfeld"
18 ___ populo (before the public)
20 "The ___ Love": Jolson
21 Toward the mouth
22 Sister of Euterpe
23 Well-apprised
24 Item in a chest
25 Catch some Z's
26 Source of sky waves
27 FOUR HORSES
31 Wood preservative
32 Norma Rae, to Sally
33 A March sister
34 Magazine VIPs
35 Put in a pet
36 Wizened
37 Aunt Bee's nephew
39 PC monitor
42 Brake part
43 Down quickly
44 Carter discovered his tomb
45 Queens stadium
46 FOUR HORSES
53 Large moth
54 "X-Files" sighting
55 Choose
56 Ukraine seaport
57 Paul's cousin on "Mad About You"
58 Linda of "Another World"
60 Just
61 Excalibur's handle
62 FOUR HORSES
69 "___ Be So Nice to Come Home To"
70 Painter Schiele
71 Disney dog
72 Long in "Boyz N the Hood"
73 Detective Lupin
75 Bando of baseball
76 Peccadillo
77 Mardi Gras follower
78 THREE HORSES
84 Towel marking
85 Attend a play
86 Murder
87 Delhi title
88 Prof.'s aides
89 Catch wind of
91 Lincoln in-law
92 Bond rating
93 Sprint competitor
96 French novelist
97 Deianira's supposed rival
98 In high spirits
100 FOUR HORSES
106 Astrologer Sydney
107 Gran Canaria, for one
108 Fontanne's better half
109 Widened at the top
110 Grub
111 Inert gas
112 Italian director Petri
113 Signs a lease
114 Act the gadfly
115 Trampled down
116 Peddle
117 Chirac's state

DOWN

1 Like hen's teeth
2 "Apollo 13" director
3 Muslim decrees
4 Author Puzo
5 Liquefy a gel
6 Harden
7 "The Biggest Little City in the World"
8 Reach a total
9 Pamper
10 Got up
11 Hedge design
12 "___ Burning": Plain
13 Philosopher Bentham
14 Sheikdom of song
15 "Family" regular Thompson
16 Of the ears
17 Quiet spot
19 Emancipator
28 Pack on the move
29 Word on a Scandinavian stamp
30 In low spirits
36 "Get lost!"
37 Like a swagman
38 Ultimate
39 Chided
40 Old Brazilian coins
41 Avenger King
42 "Harper Valley ___"
43 "The African Queen" novelist
44 Long-snouted beast
45 Crustacean feature
46 Gendarme
47 Disney head?
48 English examiners
49 Not the pick of the litter
50 Engine noise
51 Reacted to fireworks
52 Instruct
58 Intimidate
59 Eve born Eunice Quedens
60 Marshy area
63 Fertile soil
64 Slack-jawed
65 Midway prize
66 Vernacular
67 Trig ratio
68 Bartholomew Cubbins' 500
73 Eight, to Ernst
74 Three-toed bird
76 Used a firehouse pole
77 Chabrier's "Le Roi malgré ___"
79 Ryder Cup team
80 Nobelist von Baeyer
81 Sang a la Slim Whitman
82 Sarah's son
83 Bounty hunter
89 Cheer for Hollywood
90 Sushi selection
91 See 9 Across
92 Arthur Schnitzler play
93 "Breaker ___" (1979)
94 Steep-faced ridge
95 Least active
96 Welterweight champ of 1946
97 Ice house
98 Labor ___ vincit (Oklahoma motto)
99 Royal reception
100 Negri in "Forbidden Paradise"
101 Fujairah's gulf
102 Give a caveat
103 "You ___ heard nothin' yet"
104 Patron
105 When halls are decked

66 INSOUCIANT   by Gayle Dean
An original theme from our laid-back North Carolinian.

ACROSS

1 Sign of fall
6 Bowler's score
11 Boutique
15 Tampico home
19 Sign of spring
20 Musical counterpoint
21 Wailing cry
22 Old Ironsides' commander
23 Nonchalant
25 Comrade
26 Nuncupative
27 Genetic carrier
28 Short and sweet
29 Jurist Warren
31 Novelist Jong
32 Hang back
34 Nonchalant
37 Latitude
39 Reflection
41 Globes
42 Confederate general Jubal
43 Fulminate
44 Realm of Menelaus
47 Corf contents
50 Gardner in "Mogambo"
51 Earthmovers
54 Bristles
55 Metric weight
56 Succor
58 Steinbeck title word
59 Punctuation mark
61 Wireless
62 Israeli seaport
64 "Call Me ___" (1953)
65 Most secure
66 Nonchalant
72 Tilted
73 Aches
74 Abate
75 Permit
76 Reveille instrument
77 Hoist the main
79 Plod
83 Sharp
84 Secure Old Glory
85 Large Capitol room
88 Madison ___
89 Commit a faux pas
90 He pulled out a plum

92 Needlefish
93 Calyx part
95 Grange
96 Covent Garden production
98 Stonewalls
99 Nonchalant
104 Roman flower goddess
105 Banish
106 "New Yorker" cartoonist
107 Briny
109 Spurs' org.
112 China shop intruder
113 Director Kenton
115 Nonchalant
118 Unemployed
119 Agave fiber
120 Kukla's friend
121 Ben Hogan rival
122 Lachrymal secretion
123 Hetty Sorrel's love
124 Valleys
125 Crowds

DOWN

1 "Courage" singer
2 Armenia's neighbor
3 Two-sided
4 Court judge
5 End-table items
6 Frightening
7 So-so scores for Norman
8 Feed the kitty
9 Caviar
10 Make beloved
11 On-the-ball
12 "Maybe Baby" singer
13 Temple mascot
14 Layer
15 Refrain
16 Goldfinger
17 Derelict
18 Ease
24 Out of this world
30 Follows the crowd
31 Napoleon's island
33 Belter's tool
34 He discovered Mars
35 Bridge expert
36 Rover's dinner
37 Rachel's sister
38 Hangover?
39 Donated
40 Mechanic's ___
43 Copland ballet
45 Rice dish
46 Scent
47 Harmony
48 Jack
49 Show feeling
52 Salome danced for him
53 Computer adjunct
55 Boo-boos
57 George C. Scott role
60 Probability

61 Tanner's quest
63 Ball of yarn
64 Junk ___
65 Burn
66 Eccentric one
67 Merchant ship
68 Canadian physician: 1849–1919
69 Jilt
70 Quarter bird
71 Bremen negatives
76 Rangoon's land
77 Headliner
78 Nimbus
80 Sami
81 Spoon-shaped
82 Hardens
84 Shape
86 Curved molding
87 Flabbergast
90 Man without a country

91 "The Secret of ___ Inish" (1995)
94 Cochlea locale
95 Unnewsy news
97 Computer programming language
98 Criticize
99 Kind of card
100 Seep
101 Country estate
102 Black Sea resort
103 Mousse ingredient
104 Galas
107 Golfer Brett
108 Uppercut landing area
110 Solder line
111 Puts two and two together
113 They banned DDT
114 Eliminate
116 Ailing
117 Wheelhouse dir.

ACROSS

1 Style
8 Austere
15 Hockey legend Phil's nickname
19 Red-faced
20 Oregon city
21 Footprint
22 Henry James novel
25 Colombia city
26 Punta del ___, Uruguay spa
27 Aleta's son
28 Wine cask
29 Novelist May
31 "The Partridge Family" star
32 Curie and Corelli
35 Expunge (with "out")
38 ___ la journé (all day)
39 Teases
40 Word of triumph
42 Bambi's aunt
43 Avow
44 Emeril's secret
47 Neil Simon play
50 City in Holland
51 Pongids
52 Andrea ___ Sarto
54 Conduits
55 Word with note or pay
57 Abundant sources
59 Poe poem
61 Oxford width
63 Controversial spray
66 Function
67 Song hit of 1892
70 Fatuous
72 "___ Rosenkavalier"
73 One-armed bandit's arm
74 Düsseldorf neighbor
76 Marcel Marceau role
77 Film director Litvak
79 Whiskey cocktail
83 Aussie bird
84 Ward in "Killer Rules"
85 That, in Toledo
87 Blubber
88 Sardine
90 Drudge
92 Borscht ingredients
94 German connective
96 Usher follower
97 Wood sorrel
99 Michael Douglas film
102 Approved
104 "The Mummy's ___" (1944)
106 Seaborg's org.
107 Haliaeetus albicilla
108 Rude one
109 "Catch-22" actor
110 Before cloth or leaf
112 Flat-picks
114 Phoenix eager
117 Most inexperienced
119 Queen Latifah's music
121 Rock Hudson's given name
122 Henry VIII's second
123 Fossil suffixes
124 Al Smith's campaign song of 1928
130 Kind of egg
131 "A rose is ___ in the bud": Lyly
132 Lived
133 Film terrier
134 Rainmakers, at times
135 It's chewed on Broadway

DOWN

1 Handled clumsily
2 Humble
3 Inclement
4 "Days of Grace" author
5 Midwest city, for short
6 Kind of party
7 Mystery writers' awards
8 ___ Bernardino
9 Attention getter
10 Ave ___ vale
11 Most like an orb
12 Melodic syllable
13 Demeanor
14 Glasgow negatives
15 Money held in trust
16 Football play
17 Jai-alai balls
18 They have their say
23 Cycle starter
24 Magic star
30 Perplexed
32 Tourist's need
33 Like fine wine
34 Tail
36 Occupied
37 Mai ___
39 Originate
41 Shade of blue
44 Beach shelters
45 Neuter
46 TV series of 1995
47 Annapolis freshman
48 Maple genus
49 London's "___ Wolf"
53 They're found in écoles
56 O-___ ("The Good Earth" wife)
58 Normandy city
60 Standard
62 Sheena from Scotland
64 Enliven
65 Supposed
68 Actress Bonham Carter
69 "___, sure!"
71 London's ___ of Court
75 Pub offering
78 ___ kwon do
80 Aid
81 ___ Dame
82 Firefighters, at times
86 More capable
89 Cornice, for one
91 Olympic star in 1936
93 Conducted
95 Ruin
97 Wind instrument
98 Clerics
100 Terhune dog
101 Parisian preposition
103 Ring highlights
105 Sonora snooze
108 Kind of market
111 Cement
113 Set-to
114 Spiteful
115 "___ Milk Wood": Dylan Thomas
116 Poor
118 Hardy girl
120 Waterfront sight
122 A ___ apple
125 Wonder
126 Get it
127 No and Who
128 Dry, to vintners
129 Double this for a fly

68 SUPPORTING STARS   by William Canine
Small-screen luminaries shine once more below.

ACROSS

1 AARP members
4 Outback bird
7 Perspire
12 Arena sign
15 Alice worked in his diner
18 Egyptian coin
20 Reckon
21 Rich ice cream
23 E Indian sailors
24 "Home Improvement" star
25 "Bonanza" actor
26 Additionally
27 James Dean's last film
29 Burro's tail
31 Missile
32 Proofer's notation
33 Conclude
34 North Sea feeder
35 "Fish Magic" painter
36 Swarms
38 "77 Sunset Strip" actor
44 Contemn
45 Minor role
47 More down-at-heel
48 French Bourbon?
49 Square-dance
53 Roman holiday
54 Line dances
57 Opposed
58 Bishop's cap
60 Dumas blade
62 Rose fruit
64 Galba's predecessor
65 "F Troop" actor
66 Close ___ (near miss)
67 Bustle
68 Corn or pod prefix
69 Stillwater school
70 Rel. institution
71 "Ben-___"
72 Nib
74 Vapor
77 Ballerina Shearer
79 Tenor Carreras
80 Padua neighbor
81 Caterpillar, for one
82 Serpent
83 Protected
84 Suspects
86 Maternal aunt, e.g.
88 Least distinct
90 Coquettish
91 Talks twaddle
93 Steeple ornament
94 Roll cloud
97 "Murphy Brown" actor
99 Sordid
103 Bring up
104 Blubber
105 Stylishness
107 Ice sheet
108 Color
109 NASCAR's Bobby
112 Rigg in "The Avengers"
114 "M*A*S*H" star
115 Asked in
117 Did a double take
119 Journals
121 Shore
122 Prospero's sprite
123 It's higher than K2
124 PAT preceders
125 La Seyne-sur-___
126 Serving dish
127 Part of R&R
128 Hordeolum

DOWN

1 Tom Hanks film
2 Theater district
3 Mouths off
4 Greek letter
5 Combine
6 Bearlike
7 "Golden Girl" Dorothy's ex
8 Painter Kuhn
9 Addition
10 Porter and stout
11 Daly in "Cagney & Lacey"
12 Plunks
13 "Other Voices, Other ___"
14 Sphere
15 Mental condition
16 Steak au poivre, e.g.
17 Father of antiseptic surgery
19 "Joanie Loves Chachi" actor
22 "The Mary Tyler Moore Show" actor
28 Applies a rider
30 Sambar
37 Caesar
39 Exempt
40 Star of "Min and Bill"
41 NFL stats
42 Coolidge and Hayworth
43 "___ the Red, White and Blue . . .": Coward
44 Lamont, to Fred
46 "Happy Days" actor
48 "The Dick Van Dyke Show" actress
49 Belgrade river
50 Unity
51 Furrowed
52 Noon naps
54 Sheltered
55 Harmonica feature
56 Mates
59 More loyal
61 Jewish sectarian
63 Hale's "Perry Mason" role
73 "Gunsmoke" actor
75 Turn away
76 Hysterical
77 Alma ___
78 "The Life of Riley" undertaker
79 He supported 114 Across
85 Call for aid
87 Macao coin
89 U.K. solons
91 Dollops
92 Bristles
94 Talented one
95 Checked
96 Needlepoint mesh
97 Think over
98 Over there
100 Triple Entente
101 Eschewing praise
102 Frothy
104 "Blue ___ Shoes"
106 Unworldly
110 "Redigo" star
111 ___ avis
112 Profound
113 How praters talk
116 Conway or 24 Across
118 Dickens character
120 NRC forerunner

69 SHOW TUNES by Elsie Jean
Some memorable songs from the Great White Way.

ACROSS

1 Persian monarch
5 Scot's name
9 Sagan or Sandburg
13 Black dogs
17 Michael Crichton film
18 "Burr" author
20 Intaglio
21 Ocular layer
22 Not give ___ about
23 "Carousel" tune
25 City SW of Bogota
26 Speak hoarsely
27 Devoured
28 San Marino coins
29 Proficiency
30 Cast
32 Armadas
34 Hawthorne's house had seven
35 "___ to Remember"
36 Hank of hair
37 "Ziegfeld Follies" star
39 Crystalline
42 Overwhelmed
43 Naples neighbor
44 Pronto!
48 "Botany Bay" coauthor
49 One-armed bandit
50 "Alice" director
51 "Daily Planet" reporter
52 Running wild
53 Alpine pass
54 Death's-head
55 "Common Sense" author
56 Malibu hue
57 Jack salmon
58 Litter
59 Hook's partner
60 Jots
61 Orinoco tributary
62 Poet Dickinson
64 Snowplow targets
67 Dione, e.g.
69 Agatha Christie, e.g.
70 Corvine cry
73 Indian princess
74 BMI rival
75 Magder in "Rugged Gold"
76 Gaucho weapon
77 Fairy-tale fiend
78 Crazy as ___
79 Uptight state
80 Oomph
81 Pare
82 Stupefy
83 Biotite
84 Blue ribbon
85 Labellum
87 Rugged ridge
89 Mr., in Calcutta
90 Sound purchase?
93 Strauss opera
95 Caliber
99 Four-time Wimbledon winner
100 Baritone Gobbi
101 Margate is one
102 "Take Me Home" singer
103 Exude
104 "Babes in Arms" tune
108 Quasimodo's creator
109 German ice queen
110 S Nigerian city
111 Capitulate
112 La Belle Epoch et al.
113 Knock off
114 "Jenny" star
115 "Buffalo ___"
116 Disney chipmunk

DOWN

1 Precipice
2 Hourly
3 David's commander
4 "South Pacific" tune
5 Birdhouse
6 English elevators
7 Actress McClurg
8 Mount Russell loc.
9 Citadel student
10 Director Heckerling
11 Pierce Arrow contemporary
12 Costello of comedy
13 "Guys and Dolls" tune
14 Make use of
15 "Beauty and the Beast" role
16 "Red ___ in the Sunset"
19 Lounged
20 Roman Demeter
24 Competes
29 ___ Marcos
31 Drop a stitch
32 Excoriate
33 "The King and I" tune
34 Smile
36 "Damn Yankees" tune
38 Antoine Pevsner's birthplace
39 Talk
40 Mongolian monk
41 Carolina college
42 Greetings from Don Ho
43 Cerulean
45 Chimed in
46 Last Stuart queen
47 Earl, for one
49 Dumfries denizens
50 Home of the "Beacon Journal"
54 Whip
55 Blanched
57 Sheep shed
58 Mr. Scratch
59 Bound
60 "West Side Story" tune
63 Novelist Edgeworth
64 Big Board "adjustment"
65 Burning desire
66 Pertaining to
68 Image
70 Pension perk
71 Orchard pesticide
72 Giulini's stick
74 Utah resort
76 "Pal Joey" tune
78 Regarding
79 Setting
83 "Cats" tune
84 Brazilian parrot
86 Suffix for profit
87 Little green man
88 Magazine section
89 Bleachers
90 Throngs
91 Dravidian language
92 "Don't Cry for Me Argentina" musical
94 Entrance courts
95 Cantrip
96 Kirk's communications officer
97 Magisterial
98 Irregularly toothed
101 N.L. stadium
104 Ring org.
105 Norse death goddess
106 Run out
107 Barrister's wear

SIGN LANGUAGE   by Norman S. Wizer
Potent paronomasia from our Pennsylvania puzzler.

ACROSS

1 Stray
5 Fray
10 Lovesick
14 Shopping mecca
18 Norse anthology
19 Painter Nolde
20 At the crest
21 Biblical prophet
22 Sign in a restaurant?
25 They're in the loft
26 Obstinacy
27 "How sweet ___!"
28 Rock
29 Queen of 1000 days
30 Havana honcho
32 Mild oath
33 Eyeballed
36 Sign in a butcher shop?
41 Disturbed
42 Gave charity
43 Part of a cell
44 Animus
45 Sci. course
46 Paradise
48 Light-horse Harry
49 Sign in a deli?
54 They're sometimes put on
55 Account
56 Refuge
57 Gnome
58 In a gray way
60 Bold blokes
61 Dingo, for one
63 Besmears
64 Anglo-___
65 Hautbois
66 Short lawyers?
67 Sign in a music store?
74 Sloshed
75 Mary of Guise was one
76 Speck
77 Nabokov novel
78 It comes after all
80 Amplify
82 Tot's toe
84 Sign in a curiosity shop?
87 Prepares the salad
88 ___ Mater
89 Litter ones
90 Afternoon in Arras
91 Villain
94 "Diagnosis Murder" costar
95 Of no avail
99 Encore!
100 Sign in an optometrist's office?
103 "Peer Gynt" composer
104 Start of an Ellington title
105 Type of tactics
106 Reduced
107 Lip
108 Part of VIP
109 "60 Minutes" correspondent
110 Ratio words

DOWN

1 Networks
2 Together, to Barenboin
3 Pastoral poem
4 Trumpet blare
5 Video-store request
6 Satisfactory
7 Ampule
8 Tarzan portrayer
9 Burdette of baseball
10 Spat
11 "Scourge of God"
12 Porter's "Anything ___"
13 Int. disclosure
14 Harries
15 Fizzy wine
16 Composer Janáček
17 Female bairn
21 Applied, as opposed to theoretical
23 Conceded
24 Lent a hand
28 Bound
30 Cam ___ (famed harness horse)
31 "___ had it!"
32 Duplicity
33 Spanker
34 Rookie
35 Cyclist Zuelle
36 Cranny's partner
37 Crows
38 Borne on the wind
39 Come on the scene
40 "The Boys of Summer" shortstop
42 Risky
45 Type of weevil
46 Playing hooky
47 Like a popinjay
50 RBIs and ERAs
51 Tallies
52 Sartre play
53 Wayans in "The Last Boy Scout"
54 "See ya!"
57 In due time
58 Serve
59 Like Hamlet's Denmark
60 "The Wind" author
61 Positivism founder
62 Rose's romeo
63 Light lunch
64 Lilac, e.g.
67 Flattered
68 Capital of Guam
69 Throws off
70 Yenta-ish
71 Price places
72 Trim a lawn
73 Comes out with
75 Ransacking
79 Equipment movers
80 ___-the-mill
81 Small British isle
82 Cool
83 Elat citizen
85 More steamed
86 Clams up
87 Sightseer
90 A little night music?
91 Bulges
92 City on the Jumna
93 Podium
94 Anger
95 F-16 letters
96 Sit-outs
97 "___ we forget . . ."
98 Sinclair rival
100 Small taste
101 CIA forerunner
102 Famed NYC building

WHAT'S MY LINE? by Fran and Lou Sabin
Hint: "And that's the way it is . . ." is not the answer to 50 Across.

ACROSS

1 Pro ___ (proportionately)
5 Kiss from Charo
9 Interdiction
12 Throw ___ into (frighten)
18 Off to one side
19 Zulu's language group
20 Hubbub
21 Oklahoma Indians
22 Maxwell Smart line
25 Honeymoon, for some
26 Leafstalks
27 Tropical vines
29 Jugs
30 Pick over
31 Literary lead
32 Took necessary steps?
34 Big leagues
37 Dummkopfs
38 Screens
41 Adjoins
42 Steve McGarrett line
44 Innovative
45 Audience reaction
46 ___-Norwegian (Bokmal)
47 Give a shove
48 Year in the reign of Louis XII
49 Pensioned: Abbr.
50 Walter Cronkite line
54 "Qui desiderat ___": Vegetius
55 Female hormone
57 Substantial
58 Dudley and Roger
59 Appalachian Trail user
60 Bumps off
61 Teammate of 42 Down
62 Pancakes
64 Berry of "Losing Isaiah"
65 Idolized
68 "___ but a walking shadow . . .": Shak.
69 Lawrence Welk line
71 Tasha of "Star Trek: TNG"

72 "Fort Apache" actor
73 Traveller's alert
74 Snoopy's supper
75 Pop of rock
76 Charles S. Dutton show
77 Superman line
81 Accustom
82 Bohemianism
84 Favorite Van Gogh spot
85 Hunter
86 Hit hard
87 Raising the roof
88 Tobogganed
89 Pismire
91 Telecommunications satellite
93 Pest control
97 Netminder
99 Theo Kojak line
101 Wanted no part of
102 ___ Mochis
103 Spanish ladies
104 Ben in "So Big"
105 Gather again
106 Windsock indication
107 Inclusive abbr.
108 Thrall

DOWN

1 Grate
2 Sunblock additive
3 Civil disobedience
4 California fruits
5 Biblical tower site
6 Country Slaughter
7 Miami college
8 Point of view
9 Religion founded by Mirza Husayn Ali
10 Hersey setting
11 "The Godfather" composer
12 Canine org.

13 Bogart film
14 Grand dam
15 Steve Martin line
16 Tabula ___
17 Journal endings
19 Base on ___
23 Vera Lynn hit
24 Part of São Paulo
28 Freeload
31 Flatten
33 Melodious Murray
34 American skiing great
35 "___ Irish Rose"
36 Joe Friday line
37 Schwarzenegger role
38 Assume another's debts
39 Quay
40 Crawls, after a fashion
42 Ex-Yankee Hank

43 "La Bohème" numbers
46 Genoan magistrates
48 New Zealand aborigine
50 Pair of oxen
51 Griffith of boxing
52 "He can't ___ horse from a horsefly"
53 Rock's Van ___
54 X-rated
56 More mature
58 Feline sounds
60 Milne marsupial
61 Wee
62 Barton on the battlefield
63 Austerity
64 Baskets
65 Teeter and Magoni
66 Tidal flow
67 "Hunter" star
69 Gives a kick

70 Widow's inheritance
73 Young barracuda
75 Like toadstools
77 Coalitions
78 Stuporous
79 Slaver
80 Apple-pie order
81 Author Jong
83 Mrs. Marcos
85 Tactics
87 Fictional bladesman
88 Rope fiber
89 Hungarian city
90 Touch
92 Belter's tools
93 Altar locale
94 Calendar units
95 Black
96 December 31st word
98 Bullins and Bradley
100 Caldron

72 SWEET DREAMS   by Nancy Scandrett Ross
Nancy has achieved hers—top recognition among solvers.

ACROSS

1 Nomadic Finn
5 Knight wear
10 Napoleon's sister
15 Coin of Chile
19 Twelfth Jewish month
20 "Common Sense" author
21 Solitary soul
22 Composer Khachaturian
23 OF A SINGER IN THE SHOWER . . .
27 Mozart opera setting
28 Child in Cordoba
29 Playful animal
30 Rand of letters
31 Appointments
33 Advantage
35 From stem to ___
39 Woodstock performer
40 "Stanley & ___" (1990)
41 Cameroon town
44 OF A YOUNG ATHLETE . . .
50 Scintilla
51 Adds to the pot
52 Scruffs
53 Sailors' patron saint
54 Matlock of TV
55 Guide
56 Twain's ___ Joe
57 Nagy of ballet
58 Wild grain?
59 O.T. book
60 ___ monster
61 OF A PRACTICING PIANO PUPIL . . .
71 Tolkien villains
72 Jacob's first wife
73 Peace Nobelist: 1949
74 Trade center
75 Hanna-Barbera dog
76 Cavalry sword
78 Portly
81 Force ___ (draw)
82 Glycerin lead-in
83 Foreigner
84 ___ Alto
85 OF A SANDLOT SLUGGER . . .
89 Cinnabar, for one
90 River to the Baltic
91 Knocks
92 One of the Mitfords
93 Slopes transport
94 Germ cell
96 Sch. subject
98 Basso Cesare
101 Thailand, once
102 Err at the bank
107 OF A LEAD IN THE COLLEGE PLAY . . .
112 Road to Rome
113 Clamor
114 Improve
115 French infinitive
116 Infrequent
117 Low cards
118 Seeks
119 Observed

DOWN

1 Permits
2 African succulent
3 Sound of contentment
4 Entreaty
5 Put on
6 Memorable Israeli statesman
7 Spanish surrealist
8 ___ shoestring
9 Fr. relative
10 Jack Point's beloved
11 Advances
12 Word of division
13 French seasoning
14 Pitching stat
15 Agreements
16 Part of Q.E.D.
17 Store event
18 Pitcher Olivares
24 Guam capital
25 "___ of Old Smokey"
26 "El Capitan" composer
31 Household appliance
32 Benefaction
33 Smooth feathers
34 Shadow sites
35 Try
36 Ubiquitous bag
37 Deep black
38 Sleep stage
39 Essen elder
40 Attribute
41 Soprano Mosca
42 Gore Vidal's "Visit to ___ Planet"
43 Discordant-sounding
45 Durban's province
46 "And ___ grow on!"
47 Kind of circle or sanctum
48 Louisiana-style cookin'
49 "Psycho" star
55 Sun over Seville
56 Moscow locale
61 Beefsteak ___
62 Cicero or Pericles
63 "Adrienne Lecouvreur" playwright
64 Cosmetician Lauder
65 Long, heavy overcoat
66 Aquarium fish
67 Billiards shot
68 Lonesome George
69 Worth in "Orders to Kill"
70 Stray
75 Prepared to fire
76 Incline
77 Ventilates
78 "The Afternoon of a ___": Debussy
79 Evelyn Waugh's brother
80 Canadian Conservative
82 Joint in a stem
83 Partly open
84 Love's org.
86 Clive in "Frankenstein"
87 Scent
88 Choleric
93 Salisbury attraction
94 Spacek in "Three Women"
95 Steps
96 Occasion
97 Grinds
98 Ado
99 Speck
100 Wide-mouthed pitcher
101 French silk
102 Baker's need
103 Colors
104 Anatomical network
105 Interlaken river
106 Small songbird
108 Busy insect
109 Neither follower
110 Cowgirl's cry
111 Cassowary's relative

73 GALLICISMS by Randolph Ross
Parlez-vous Français?

ACROSS

1 Cow catcher
6 S.A. rodent
10 In the Land of Nod
16 Easy gait
17 ___ Bator
18 Erudite
20 Done deal
22 Got one's hackles up
24 Say with conviction
25 Duplicated
26 Liability
27 Widespread
28 Middle, to Spence
29 Thimhu loc.
30 "___ hell": Sherman
32 Parking sticker
33 First family's residence
34 Revolution
36 Bridge combination
37 Formerly the Belgian Congo
39 First name in fashion
40 Like a tercel
41 African soccer org.
43 Blank check
47 Battleship letters
48 "Juno and the Paycock" playwright
50 Biblical priest
51 Weeks in Madrid
53 Use a swizzle
54 Attended
55 And others
56 Go for a run
59 Skydome home
62 Airline of yore
64 100 square meters
65 Ancient Greek colony
69 Grounded birds
72 "Young Frankenstein" heroine
73 Mother-of-pearl source
74 Tennis replay
75 Go to court
77 Half a Kenyan revolutionary
79 Simpson trial, e.g.
82 It launched C. Chase
83 Syrupy
85 Noun suffix
86 Marie Louise de la Ramée
88 Relative of ltd.
89 Epicurean
92 Popular board game
95 Influenza or Ebola
96 Punny pianist
97 Author of "The Name of the Rose"
98 Street boss
99 Prince of Arabia
100 Corn bread
101 Allergic reaction
103 17th-century entertainment
104 1990 US Open tennis champ
106 High fashion
108 Merciful
109 Grimm character
110 Sounds
111 Den equipment
112 Out of commission
113 "GoodFellas" star

DOWN

1 Hands-off economic doctrine
2 Dish
3 Gawk
4 Persuasion
5 Mythical monster
6 Inflate
7 Monte Rosa, e.g.
8 "Tobacco Road" novelist
9 Black bird
10 Even though
11 Croatian neighbors
12 Café au ___
13 Hesitant utterances
14 Confidentially
15 Big-billed birds
16 Sheathed
19 Mars
20 Renown
21 Diamond Head locale
23 Struck out
26 Webb series
29 Transvaal settler
31 Welcome order to a GI
32 Wilmington loc.
34 Spiny lobster
35 Maynard's friend
36 Architectural band
38 Stolen diamonds
40 One of the Seven Sages
41 ___ del Sol
42 Trouper
44 Darjeeling
45 Freddy's street
46 Nashville org.
49 Lobby sign
52 "___ for Alibi": Grafton
54 ___ a cucumber
56 Indefinable quality
57 Grinder's instrument
58 Tree knot
60 Pinch
61 Poodle size
63 Iceberg part
66 Singer Rawls
67 Forthcoming
68 ___ things (hallucinating)
69 Gage title
70 Swimmer Stewart
71 Salt Lake athlete
73 Up-to-date
75 In ___ (stuck)
76 Kennedy Library architect
77 Barely adequate
78 Attributes to
80 Media attention
81 Statesman Sonny
83 Calls to Zapata
84 Correlatives
87 Extreme
89 Tuna look-alike
90 Kind of interest
91 Need aspirin
93 Worsens
94 Patella
96 French maid
98 Adams and Frickert
100 Quay
102 Glow
103 Pout
105 Pull even
106 Bricklayer's trough
107 Fez or kepi

STEPQUOTE   by Walter Covell
Walter dedicates this to Eugene T. Maleska.

ACROSS

1 Stepquote: Part 1
5 Posture
11 Like Mardi Gras
18 She has a shower
19 Ancient Greeks
21 Author of stepquote
22 Ligament
23 Cheshire Cat, for one
24 Gulf of Genoa port
25 Board the Orient Express
27 Give the go-ahead
28 Convex moldings
30 Stagers
31 Stepquote: Part 3
33 Mexican medicinal plant
36 Fundamentals
40 Algerian port
42 ITAR-___ news agency
43 Platonistic idea
47 Many-sided
50 Macho
52 Virginia willows
53 Pump
54 Some have crowns
57 Famed Dadaist
58 Fits companions
60 Stepquote: Part 5
62 Half a table game
63 ___ B'rith
64 Pays up
66 Approached evasively
68 Tabula ___
69 Harvest
70 Marks paper, in a way
71 Lowdown
73 Suburb of Padua
76 Ingle enhancers
78 Having a schnozz
82 Cop a look
83 "Rosamond" composer
84 Stepquote: Part 7
87 "Waiting to ___" (1995)
88 Claire in "Claudia"
89 Most perceptive
91 Mirror backing
93 Statesman De Valera
94 Mount Saint Helens' range
96 Patronages
99 Terrific bargain
100 Eskers
102 "A Fish Out of Water" fish
103 Away from the wind
104 Makes alcohol undrinkable
108 Stepquote: Part 9
110 Summit
113 Cygnet genus
114 Take to court
116 In theory
121 Stove pail of yore
123 "Unforgiven" star
126 Land of Cotton
127 Corral
128 Woodworking job
129 Horace, for one
130 More precipitous
131 Afts
132 Stepquote: Conclusion

DOWN

1 Triplet
2 Intimation
3 Fulda tributary
4 Stepquote: Part 2
5 Ladies of Rome
6 Craggy peak
7 Blue dye
8 Diamond groups
9 A choral work
10 Polyethyl ending
11 Iron: Comb. form
12 AOL letter
13 Certain IRA
14 Toil
15 Fair or Lundy
16 Manège movement
17 Adam's grandson
18 "Mad cow" disease
20 Young Sp. ladies
26 Pedestal figure
29 "___ bodkins!"
32 Stepquote: Part 4
34 Emollient
35 Fisheye ___
36 Faulty
37 Montana city
38 Gangway gripper
39 Gene Roddenberry creation
41 Glowing gas
44 Goddess of the hunt
45 Gumbos
46 Cuttlefish genus
48 Basket fiber
49 Stick anew
50 Pale-green insect
51 Embattled forest in WW2
55 Comical penguin
56 Sass
59 Merman's mate
61 Stepquote: Part 6
63 Hubbub
65 Meager
67 Explorer or car
70 AAA suggestions
72 Hellman's "The Little ___"
73 De Mille films
74 French legislature
75 Ruffle the hair
77 Vane dir.
79 Dravidian of India
80 Abscond
81 Compact
85 Billionth: Comb. form
86 Stepquote: Part 8
89 Welt
90 Ivan or Peter
92 Some are sweet
95 Grain beetle
97 In attendance
98 Artery
100 Western Indian
101 Catches a wave
105 Slipknot
106 Winterberry
107 Glove leather
109 Stepquote: Part 10
110 King takers
111 Eur. or Afr.
112 Defensive spray
115 Eastern potentate
117 Helper
118 XXXI x II
119 The Mikado had one
120 Still
122 Short trip
124 Headland
125 Bay State cape

COUNTDOWN   by Sam Bellotto Jr.
Start at 23 Across and work your way to 114 Across. A-OK?

ACROSS

1 Balderdash!
4 Part of A.M.P.A.S.
8 Sings jazzily
13 Brilliance
18 Deet-banning agcy.
19 "Traffic" star
20 Up in ___ (undecided)
22 They're often girded
23 Taxi dancer's fare, at one time
25 Convict's objective
26 Rolling Stones hit
27 Highlight of 2 Down
28 RPM instrument
30 Hugh Grant comedy
32 Of the stomach
34 Olive in a Caesar salad?
36 French Foreign Legion member
37 River City game
39 Island in the Seine
40 Child or Pence
43 Frog or toad
46 Sought office
47 Bankroll
48 Ring-shaped reef
49 Marital malaise
53 Principal's deg.
55 Charlottesville col.
56 Avoid
57 Stewed
58 ___ polloi
59 Get rid of
61 Shooter ammo
62 Musketeers motto word
63 "Candid Camera" host
64 Holiday music
65 Top brass
70 Ranking monastic
72 Prefix for flavin
73 Portuguese pronoun
74 LIRR stop
77 Like some stop signs
79 Suffix for Capri
80 Adjust a skirt
81 "Do You Know What ___": Lee Michaels hit
83 West of Sask.
84 French soul

85 "Joy to the World" group
88 Home in the hills
90 Song syllables
92 ___ Friday
93 Look the other way
94 "___ bien!"
95 Anti-smoking org.
96 Like tyrannosaurs
99 Ropes on the range
101 "Ich bin ___ Berliner": Kennedy
102 Galley slaves
106 Amateur hour attraction
108 TV's "Quick ___ McGraw"
110 Louisiana town
111 Scacchi in "Turtle Beach"
112 Obstructed, once
114 Countdown conclusion
116 Cianfrocco of baseball
117 Dhamar denizen
118 Write up a speeder
119 Upstate NY school
120 "The Old ___ Bucket"
121 Like the Aesir
122 Hair of the dog bee
123 Faline's mother

DOWN

1 Mark differently
2 "Irmelin" or "Koanga"
3 Ancient city of Lower Egypt
4 Put down a hero
5 First major U.S. battle of WW1
6 Cement
7 LP or CD
8 Letters on an Indy car

9 She made "No. 5" famous
10 Lofty
11 French breeze
12 European coal region
13 Twisted-horn antelope
14 Get in touch with
15 Pharos
16 Spanish liqueur
17 Half a fly
21 Shaped anew
24 Wedding worker
29 Tasmanian capital
31 Corrida cheer
33 Laughing
35 Wool: Comb. form
38 "Happy ___ to You": Evans song
41 "One Night" singer
42 Source of linen
43 PDQ relative
44 High mountain snow
45 Tunic of the eye
47 Beatles' album

48 "A Passage to India" heroine
50 "Cosmopolitan" competitor
51 "The 13 Clocks" author
52 Michael Crichton book
54 Winger in "Forget Paris"
60 Coin of Kabul
62 Sci-fi writer Davidson
63 Religion
65 Soft wood
66 Hawkeye
67 Harness races
68 Cleopatra's ___
69 Dagwood's neighbor
70 Pivotal
71 Gawk at
74 State flower of Utah
75 Himalayan goat
76 Pay to play
77 Actuality

78 Staunch
80 Mended
81 Stevens in "Madigan"
82 Attitude
86 Painter Schiele
87 Super power?
89 "___ Light": The Five Americans hit
91 Dinosaur
95 One ___ time
96 Camper
97 Does a road job
98 Vezina Trophy winner
100 With full force
103 "Indecent Proposal" star
104 Mischievous
105 Pact signed by Bush and Clinton
106 Odd, in Orkney
107 Vapor: Comb. form
109 Erythrocytes: Abbr.
111 City in Mali
113 Cross the Styx
115 Red or Dead

ANSWERS

#1

```
CORA    GOGO    FACE
GELID  NOVATO   OCHS
ELIDE  ADEMON   UTAN
SEVENDOWN  MELROSE
TBA  ALMA  PIASTRE
   TURISTA   CUE
 ASHE  AWNER  ENDS
TSHIRTS  ONTO  NOAH
ICER  HEADERS  DOVE
COST  REDO  ESTONIA
STAY  EREWE   OWED
   ALE  ANDLOAN
 DECADAL  WORD  ZAG
BARRIOS  SIXTYDOWN
ARNO  WAHINE  IONIA
MISS  NISNAS  SMART
ANTS    RTES   HOLE
```

#2

```
ASSTS   NAOMI   PESTO
NITRO   EDWIN   ALERT
ODEON  CONNECTICUT
NEWYORK   CROSS
    ARAL  SETS  EARN
MONTANA  WRITE  GAR
ALE   ACTA  ARIZONA
REACT  ERTE  ENO
COLORADO  ILLINOIS
   MIR  TARO  GELEE
ALABAMA  BENS   ERR
LIP  LABEL  GEORGIA
PLOT  DYNE  ERGO
   AMASS   VERMONT
MISSISSIPPI   EAGER
ABETS  ELIOT  SIEVE
NONET  SEEPY  SNEES
```

#3

```
APACHE  CEASE  STEN
DOODAD  ARGON  AWAY
MERRYGOROUND  RITA
ITT  SECEDE  IRISES
TSAR  TEE  TVA  TRA
   AMEER  GHETTO
 DEFECT  PER  SOFIA
FALTER  AUTO  EFTS
AYE  TURNTABLE  CAP
TACT  EDIT  ANNALS
ENTRY  SEN  SNOOPY
   REACTS  ANGST
AMI  LAS  PRE  ERGS
SOCCER  AENEAS  ERE
SOFA  POTTERSWHEEL
ERAS  EVERT  TARSAL
TENT  DONAT  ONSETS
```

#4

```
JUDEA  OPTS   TRACE
UDALL  LOOIE  RAMAL
GOLFBALLSVELOCITY
    LEDA  CALIPERS
HOMIER  MAN  PHD
ARAK  ISM  MAI  POG
SIZEOFTENNISCOURT
PGA  ETI  ABLE  ARGO
   TAR  LOCAL  ORC
SELL  STAR  IER  HUG
PLATETOSECONDBASE
YAN  LEN  ONT  ESSE
   TEA  EFT  AUGERS
 ROOMMATE  SILO
HOCKEYSTICKLENGTH
OATEN  HANOI  NINES
GRANT   STEP  TAUNT
```

#5

```
M A M B A . A B A S H . S H A R I
O L E I N . G R E T E . P E N A L
A L L E Z V O U S E N . A R T I E
. A R I A . T O P . I N D E N T .
C O N S O L E . P I C A S S O . .
S K I . I V Y . N A G . . M I B .
A D N A U S E A M . R O M A N C E
. . S S E . H A K E . O N I O N .
L O A T H . M O N E T . D I A N E
A L L E E . A O N E . N E T . . .
S P A R R E D . A L M A M A T E R
T E M . E R S . Y A P . O N O . .
. A N D R E W S . T O N N A G E .
A P I A R Y . E W E . L A O S . .
R U S S E . A D I N F I N I T U M
A L O H A . S E N N A . A R E N A
M I N E D . K N E A D . S E D A N
```

#6

```
. C R A B . S U M A C . S U A V E
D E E R E . A R I T H . A N G E R
U N B A L L O I N M A S C H E R A
O T E L L O . S T O R M . A N D S
S O L . R O K S . M O U N T I E .
. . . T R I B . E G A D . . . . .
L U I S A M I L L E R . R Y A N .
I N N A T E . E E L S . . M A B .
S T O R E R . G A D . R E M A D E
T E N . M A N E . E L A T E D . .
. R E L Y . I L T R O V A T O R E
. . E A R S . . R E N E . . . . .
O C T O P U S . S H A N . A L A .
L Y O N . I H A T E . G U S S E T
L A F O R Z A D E L D E S T I N O
I N U R E . P E A L E . M A D A M
E S S A Y . E N D O W . A Y E S .
```

#7

```
S T E P . B U R R O S . F O A M S
I S L A . I N S A N E . U N C I A
F A I R W E A T H E R F R I E N D
T R A D E R S . M E A L . T I N .
. . O S S . A C I N G . L A V E .
S C A N T . L I L L E . F A T E S
I O N S . P E K O E . E L D E R S
T A N . P O M E S . A T E E . . .
S T E A L S O N E S T H U N D E R
. G A I N . C A T E R . A X E . .
D E C E I T . M A L A R . D R A B
E L A N D . P A L E R . T E E M S
B E R T . R A I L S . S O L . . .
A V A . B A R T . S T R A I T S .
S A V E S F O R A R A I N Y D A Y
E T A P E . L E G A T E . E L A N
D E N I S . E D A M E S . D E L E
```

#8

```
I O W A N . S L A B . A C C E P T
B R A V O . T I M E . B E A N I E
M O T O R . S T O R M C E N T E R
. . E N D S . H U G O . . A R C S
A P R . I C I E R . O N A . E E E
D E F A C E D . S T R E S S E D .
E A R P . N O D . O S A K A . . .
S H O P . A L A M O . R E M O V E
T E N E T . S M O T E . R O P E S
E N T A I L . P O L I O . V E R S
. S N A R E . E G G . A N N A . .
. S T E E L E R S . H E A R S A Y
P A R . S A P . A N T E D . D L S
S L O E . I O T A . S O S O . . .
H A P P Y E N D I N G . P O O L S
A M E E R S . O R C A . T Y R O L
W I S E S T . R E E D . S A S S Y
```

#9

```
H A R R I S . B A T . S H I L L
A V A U N T . S O L A . E E R I E
J E F F E R S O N A I R P L A N E
I S T O . E L S E . A T O N E S .
. . U T O P I A . A D I T . . . .
F L A S H C A D I L L A C . W E D
I A M . E E L . A I R . T A L E .
T R A U M A . B I B . M U S I C .
. . V A N M O R R I S O N . . . .
Q U E E N . I D A . E T A P E S .
U L N A . D N A . M N O . I C E .
O U T . R E O S P E E D W A G O N
. . S E C T . I N H A N D . . . .
A T H E N A . S C U T . . O R C A
G R A N D F U N K R A I L R O A D
R O U S E . N I L E . N E E D L E
A D L E R . E T E . A S S E S S
```

#10

```
. N E S S . B O A Z . O D I S T S
S E X E S . R I S E . T E A P O T
W H E N A M A N H A S T O M A K E
A R C S . I N K . L I S . B R E R
P U R E S T . C O G . . . T N N .
. A S P E E C H T H E . V A S E .
D A T . I S T A R . T R E E . . .
E B O A T . C N O . S T R A I T .
F I R S T T H I N G H E H A S T O
G E Y S E R . I I I . A S K E W .
. A R I D . C L E A N . E M S . .
T R E Y . G E R A L D F O R D . .
H E X . B E L . . A L A T E D . .
E L A M . N B A . S T S . Z O L A
D E C I D E I S W H A T T O S A Y
A N T L E R . O H I O . A R E N O
S T A T E D . N O M S . U S E D .
```

#11

```
. E S T A . C A T . S T R A F E D
A N T I C . A S E . M E A S U R E
C H A C H A C H A . A N C O N E S
L A N K . N A I L . M I F F . .
A N D . A T O P . F L E E . U S N
I C I C L E S . R U N S I N T O
M E N A G E . T R I S . T O F A T
. B E D S H E E T S . N U K E
W A S . R U N R U N R U N . N E D
I M A N . P O U N D E D O N
L A Y U P . O S E S . A R I S E R
M I S T R U S T . S T A T U R E
A N A . O N E S . C O O S . B A B
. Y E N S . T O U R . I T S A
L A S S O E S . Y E S Y E S Y E S
S T A T U E S . R U E . D U P R E
D O Y E N N E . O R D . O P E S
```

#12

```
B E R E T . S C A R A B . A H A S
E R O D E . T O L E D O . M O T T
S O L E S U R V I V O R . A L S O
T S E . S P E E . E R A L . Y E S
. R E A P . O R E . L A M A S
L A S E R S . R L S . A L A .
A S K S A . O D E S . M A C R O
U T A H . B L O C . T H A N K E D
N E T . C L A M O R O U S . E N D
C R E D I T S . D U P E . B R A E
H O B A N . S I G N . S E E M S
. O R D . M E T . C H A L E T
S P A T E . A P R . C O E D .
T A R . R A T A . D E L L . V A T
A N D Y . B A S S O R E L I E V O
I D E M . A L S A C E . A L T E R
N A D A . S L E E K S . C L O S E
```

#13

```
M A G G I O . L E V E L . P A P A
A R O U N D . I L I V E . A L E X
T I S S U E O F L I E S . T A K E
H A S . S A T E . I N S P I R E D
E N I D . B T U . E O N .
R E P A S T . O N I O N S K I N S
. D A R . A M I . H I R A M
B E S A M E . S A S S . N A P A
E R A . P A R C H M E N T . D E R
B I T S . T U L A . A R R E S T
O C U L I . D O M . R O O .
P A P E R T I G E R . K N I F E D
. E A R . D E W . L I D O
K N A P S A C K . B O O M . N S W
N O D I . C A R B O N C O P I E S
O N E L . T R I E R . T A T T L E
B O N Y . S A S I N . O B S E S S
```

#14

```
R E D S . O S C A R . A L I A S
E L I T E . B O I T E . M A M B O
T I M E I . S O R T S . A S P E N
E X P E R I E N C E I S T H E .
S I L V E R S . M D I I . R E T
T R E E . A S B . P U N . P A L E
. I R A T E . M E T E R
S L I D . A V E R . D E R I V E
N A M E E V E R Y O N E G I V E S
I M P A L E . A R I L . L E N A
P O O N A . R A N C H .
E R L E . M E T . A I T . D E C A
D E I . S A L T . L I A I S O N
. T O T H E I R M I S T A K E S
A D E L E . A R I A S . A L I D A
W I L D E . S E T I T . D E M I T
L A Y E R . E D E N S . D O T E
```

#15

```
S P U M E . C R A Z E . M A C E D
T A B O R . R A M O N . A R O M A
A D O R E . A D I O S . R A B I N
B U L L I O N I S M . N I M B L E
S A T E . R I I S . S E N I L E
. Y A L U . J O C O S E
A P B . T O M A H A W K S . S E C
L A U R E N . L A M E S . E T A L
L U C R E . L A S E R . F L O R A
A S K S . M U S T S . G R A N N Y
N E E . C O C K A I G N E . E S S
. T H A L I A . L A D E
I S O L D E . L E I S . T S A R
I D E A L S . R A M S H A C K L E
N E A R S . D I V O T . S H A D E
R A T S O . A G A T E . T E T E S
E S S E N . G A L E N . I R E N E
```

#16

```
T A O S . C A W . C O S . W A D E
A G R I . S C R E A M S . A D E N
P E A N U T H E A V E N . L A N D
E N T E R . E S S E N . U N I T E
S T E W I N . T E T . E N U R E D
. S R S . T R A C T
. A R F . A H A B . A V O C A D O
E M A I L . A B A . L E A R N E D
R U B L E . L U N G E . C E D E D
A L I B A B A . F R I . H E R D S
S E N E G A L . F O G G . K O S
. R U R A L . H A S
S I T T E R . L E T . B O L G E R
A R A B S . P A R E E . P E A L E
P E N A . A L M O N D S H A P E D
I N K Y . B E A S T I E . S E N D
D E S I . C D S . H E X . T R A Y
```

#17

```
RAPID  GORE    EDAM
ODILE  LEADTO  WEVE
AZTECWARRIOR   OSEE
DEADAIR  ATTACKERS
SSS  DREW  IOLA  RYE
     FEE  HBO  SLOT
TUBES  LIANG  LIGER
OPRY  CORY  ANILINE
REO  FULLPRICE  ASA
INKWELL  OENO  ANOD
ODEON  SERBS  MITRE
     NETS  RTE  VOX
APB  OLLA  CHET  RAP
POLONAISE  IRONORE
GOAL  SPIRALBRIDGE
ALDA  HONIED  ELIOT
REEF     GENA  DENSE
```

#18

```
DACRON  ABHOR  ABCS
AERATE  BLEND  ULAN
BRONTESAURUS  SALE
SOU  RECESS  STILE
     SUP  DUSE  GEEZER
SENATES  YEARNERS
HANDLER  OBOIST
ADEEMS  PLANT  AHAB
BASRA  SOARS  STAGE
ETTA  CHEFS  SPIREA
     CHEOPS  SHOOTER
HITHERTO  STATUES
INHERE  UNIO  SSB
PAREE  PROFIT  RAY
PROV  FIRSTCOZZENS
IONE  UNITE  LINAGE
EWER  RESOD  LASKER
```

#19

```
JESTER  PRAM  CALEB
OCTAVE  HOLE  AGILE
WHENINDOUBT  SOMME
LOA  COUNT  ACTRESS
     MAT  PIER  HEAR
HAIL  SEC  AGER  ICE
EYELET  SABER  ACER
XEROXES  BAN  ESKER
     WINTHETRICK
COVET  OAT  ENRAGED
AWED  MOIST  LUNATE
BEN  WOLF  AMY  CRAB
     ETAL  ALDA  MEG
CARAVEL  APNEA  OAF
ELATE  EDMONDHOYLE
LATER  FUEL  DALLAS
TIERS  TORE  ALDERS
```

#20

```
SAG  BLAB  CRETE  PEER
ARR  IOLA  PADUA  OMRI
LEI  BULLDOGDRUMMOND
ENZO  TIME  EAN  OPTED
MAZERS  OMAS  SUR  ESL
     LIE  ARID  SOSO  STE
BOYLA  CATSTEVENS
ERA  DEAL  AVER  ABEL
ADD  IND  CARER  BLASE
TEASED  ORSON  PRETTY
LAMAS  UNAPT  REA  MAD
ELSA  ANEW  PUNY  ATE
     BUFFALOBOB  ESSEN
VIP  ROLL  BARE  RAT
ECU  ARO  AINT  ESSENE
LATEN  WAR  TEAL  EROS
CROCODILEDUNDEE  SIT
RUNT  ENATE  DINE  OSE
OSSO  EGRET  STAG  NEE
```

#21

```
COST  TSPS  CAPE  BOLT
OLEA  ATIT  AGAS  ONEI
RICKILAKE  DISC  NOEL
NOTEDLY  DELTABURKE
     TOOL  PATE  PAS
ETHELWATERS  HER  TIS
LOONS  TORN  BASEMENT
ERR  ZEUS  MAS  EERY
CENTRE  RIVERPHOENIX
     HARM  SID  SEPT
PETEFOUNTAIN  CASTRO
ELAM  SOS  CASK  RIA
ASPERSED  MASC  CLICK
SES  END  GARTHBROOKS
     FLO  TONE  OREO
BILLYOCEAN  LOAFERS
AREA  PARD  JEANMARSH
TMAN  ERSE  DART  HIVE
HANK  DEED  RUSE  SAPS
```

#22

```
SITAR  JOYOUS  DEUCES
ADOBE  ADORNS  ARROYO
CLUBSANDWICH  TABLET
RETAIL  LEO  METAL
ARS  SCAM  LURID  NAPE
     TONES  TON  AARON
PAT  VEALSHANKS  DSO
BLOB  ENNUI  DONT  GEL
SERIF  TIER  WIRER
     STOOD  EDOTT  TAPES
ISLIP  CHAR  LOEWE
CEL  KALE  CERES  SNAP
OWL  SLICEOFPIE  SKI
MEATY  ECU  TINAS
ARCH  FRETS  TACT  AFC
HYPES  ETA  ORALIA
WEIMAR  ORANGEWEDGES
IMPUGN  SPINET  SEALE
MUSSES  SENSED  SEEDY
```

Crossword puzzle solutions

#23

RES · REMIT · · FOB · CASS
ELUCIDATES · ARA · · OMAN
DEBASEMENT · · CORNPONE
NOTRE · ERRANT · REPUTE
ENOLS · · AERO · · EVENER
COTS · CONCRETE · ARTES
KRA · CHIC · · LATISH
SAL · AENEAS · URE · EROS
· DIRK · SCARED · AURA
SITIN · ITALO · · ADREM
ODES · CANAPE · NAGS
BAAL · ORT · ATTILA · CPD
· ONEIRO · USER · OOI
CHACO · DOGMATIC · PWTS
RELATE · · RIZO · ALSAB
ACETIC · FEDORA · MALTA
CARINATE · STAGNATION
OTTO · DAS · TIGHTROPED
WEAN · SOT · CEASE · SSS

#24

ESTHER · DOPED · MARCOS
SCHIZO · ARETE · EMERGE
CREPESUZETTE · MASADA
RIP · LINZ · ARABS · SEL
OBOE · NULLO · ERE · OHNE
WEEPS · MEETS · TRASH
· STICK · MICE · SISERA
· CALICOCATS · MILAN
PDQ · LADEN · TOAD · EMIT
RAU · AUEL · ITIS · ENE
IRIS · SALE · SLOAN · TYS
ZILCH · LAWNTENNIS
ENTREE · REDO · ATEAM
· IOWAN · RALPH · SASIN
HAND · REB · KAROL · MARI
ELG · RAZOR · AREA · LAC
RUBRIC · TICKINGCLOCK
BREACH · CLUES · ORIOLE
SEETHE · HEDGE · FENNEL

#25

ABSALOM · CAMPO · ASHER
COLLODI · ATARA · CHORE
SCOLDANAUTHOR · RELAX
AGO · ELDER · · GOLD
· THROWASEINE · FUDD
PERSIA · ALT · NATE · PIE
ECU · GRAY · EVIAN · ACE
CONCHES · LABELTIMBER
OLIOS · SMITERS · DEA
SINN · OMARS · · TRIP
· TIS · FRILLED · BERRA
KNOCKKETTLE · CARDIAC
NIA · ELLAS · TIKI · ETE
ANY · GAOL · DSO · INBRED
PEKE · UNSEATKANGA
· RAGS · PRAYS · LAW
AROSE · SPONSORGELLER
BOYER · RADII · ESTELLE
SIDLE · ODETS · DACTYLS

#26

AGORA · ADAS · PASSED
COMAS · ARULE · FELLINI
TUNIS · EGEST · ATLANTA
ITISEASYTOBEBRAVE
· ENROLS · ATLI · ECOL
YOM · TAPE · CUE · UBE
ENAMELS · RAKISH · PRET
GELID · PALS · ARREST
GRID · BERIA · CAROUSES
· WOLFANDTHEKID
FIDELITY · DOORS · ELAN
ARISES · AINU · SNORE
NEST · SHINNY · DICTATE
ONA · AMI · META · FED
NEFF · ARUM · TOMATO
· FROMASAFEDISTANCE
AREOLES · TONES · ITOLD
TOCSINS · EROSE · NEMEA
METHOD · DENT · GROOM

#27

SPAS · DOIT · GAPE · MUST
LOVE · OLDE · IDEA · ONEA
ALEX · DIALMFORMURDER
VERTIGO · LET · TENTERS
· EKES · NET · STAR
BATTER · STUDER · ORCUS
UGH · AAR · RAG · SASE
THELADYVANISHES · PEW
ASININE · ODE · SWORDS
· EMIR · AMO · TATI
HECATE · ALA · CRITICS
APR · ALFREDHITCHCOCK
LIES · YES · ITE · ROO
OCTAD · DONATE · FRONTS
· ASIS · NOT · GRIP
AFGHANI · UTE · REBECCA
PLEASUREGARDEN · NULL
EENY · FALA · INEZ · ERAS
SATS · FELT · CARY · DEMO

#28

AKIND · IFNI · MIST · EST
DEFOE · CLAN · ANTEATER
DRILLCHUCK · STINGRAY
· AIL · BREST · LOREN
CHANCES · ERTE · ERE
LIV · TATA · ERAS · EMIT
UTE · IRISHSTEW · ADANO
NORA · SNOUT · DERN · RRS
GRAFT · ENROL · DONATES
· GARR · ELMOS · DALI
AMERICA · SAVOR · LEAST
RAJ · MAGI · TINES · CLIO
CLOTS · UNIONJACK · ANN
OLEO · CATS · ACHE · RAT
· LAH · ETAS · HORATIO
· ALIVE · NORTH · ONT
DRIVERED · DOUBLEBILL
SIDERITE · ERMA · LARUE
MDS · SEED · NESS · STAGG

#29

```
M A R A T   N O S I E R   S H O E D
A M E C H E   O R A N G E   H A L L E
D O C T O R Z H I V A G O   A R I S E
E R R   L I E   G O N E   C L E V E R
I O U   E N D E A R E D   H O M E
R U I N   A M Y   A I M   R E D
A S T O   A S T I   C E L T   S T A R
  D E L I   O H N O   D O W S E
A R A   D E T E C T I V E   A N I T A
T I L I N G   P A O L O   K I S S E R
O P E R A   C O M E D I A N S   T R Y
L O C K S   O D E S   B O Y S
L U G S   H E E L   N A S T   C A P S
S T U   T E D   T A R   I S L E
  I O W A   S T A C C A T O   T E A
W I N G E R   C A K E   N A H   R A P
A D E L E   H O T E L P A R A D I S O
R E S E T   A R E O L A   T R A D E R
S A S S Y   W E R N E R   E B E R T
```

#30

```
F A N S   N E W T   A V E C   T A M
I C E T   F L O E   L A N A I   E N O
T H R E E L I M E I S L A N D   A N T
S E V E R   E N L A I   T I S S U E
  D E N I S O N   I T S T O O T E A L
  K A Y   V I E W   T E L L S
T H E N A K E D P E A   I T I N
W E R E   E Z I O   A R I Z O N A N
E A R S   O L E   G L E E   A R A
E V A S   L O D E N D A Y S   S T E T
Z E N   T A P E   D R S   T U N A
E N T W I N E S   E S T A   I R A N
  O N E R   J O D I E F O R E S T
A M O U R   A M I D   A R M
R O C K O F S A G E   B R O A D E N
C U R S O R   I G O T O   H O V E L
H R A   F E E L I N G O F J A D E V U
E N C   S E V E N   I N R E   G R E G
R E Y   S E R G   F E A T   E Y R E
```

#31

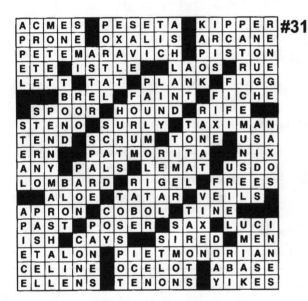

```
A C M E S   P E S E T A   K I P P E R
P R O N E   O X A L I S   A R C A N E
P E T E M A R A V I C H   P I S T O N
E T E   I S T L E   L A O S   R U E
L E T T   T A T   P L A N K   F I G G
  B R E L   F A I N T   F I C H E
  S P O O R   H O U N D   R I F E
S T E N O   S U R L Y   T A X I M A N
T E N D   S C R U M   T O N E   U S A
E R N   P A T M O R I T A   N I X
A N Y   P A L S   L E M A T   U S D O
L O M B A R D   R I G E L   F R E E S
  A L O E   T A T A R   V E I L S
A P R O N   C O B O L   T I N E
P A S T   P O S E R   S A X   L U C I
I S H   C A Y S   S I R E D   M E N
E T A L O N   P I E T M O N D R I A N
C E L I N E   O C E L O T   A B A S E
E L L E N S   T E N O N S   Y I K E S
```

#32

```
N E H I   A D S   B A W L   P O I S E
A L O T   T O I L E T R Y   E M A I L
T I M O T H Y D A L T O N   R A N D I
O S E   H E L E N   A N D E S   F R A
  S T O N E A G E   G O R I L L A S
C Y P R U S   U L M   N O S E E
R O U E   S K O K I E   S T A M P S
I N N K E E P E R   L A G   S P I R E
  S L Y E R   T A R O T   S N A G
A E R   S E A N C O N N E R Y   G M A
G L O M   D R E A M   I T E M S
R E G A L   S L R   U N H E A L T H Y
I C E C A P   S P A R G E   A A R E
  R A T E D   E N G   S N I P E S
D A M O C L E S   G E L A T I N S
U D O   H E L P S   N O M A N   I L K
K I O S K   P I E R C E B R O S N A N
E E R I E   H E A V Y S E T   O T T O
S U E T Y   I S M S   S R S   P O E T
```

#33

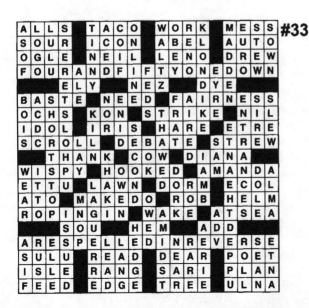

```
A L L S   T A C O   W O R K   M E S S
S O U R   I C O N   A B E L   A U T O
O G L E   N E I L   L E N O   D R E W
F O U R A N D F I F T Y O N E D O W N
  E L Y   N E Z   D Y E
B A S T E   N E E D   F A I R N E S S
O C H S   K O N   S T R I K E   N I L
I D O L   I R I S   H A R E   E T R E
S C R O L L   D E B A T E   S T R E W
  T H A N K   C O W   D I A N A
W I S P Y   H O O K E D   A M A N D A
E T T U   L A W N   D O R M   E C O L
A T O   M A K E D O   R O B   H E L M
R O P I N G I N   W A K E   A T S E A
  S O U   H E M   A D D
A R E S P E L L E D I N R E V E R S E
S U L U   R E A D   D E A R   P O E T
I S L E   R A N G   S A R I   P L A N
F E E D   E D G E   T R E E   U L N A
```

#34

```
S A B U   S E R E   G E N A   F O A M
I R O N   E G A N   L O O S   I N M Y
P U L L I N G S T R I N G S   T I E R
S T O O L S   H I E D   S I N A T R A
  C L A M   R E E F   S O S
P I C K S T U N E S   E N T R A N T S
U N A   E T O   E L L E   A F O U L
B A L L A D E E R   E L A N   I N G A
  S L O W   S L A M S   R E D D E S T
  W E B   S P A T S   W E D
A C C E D E D   P E E P S   F L A P
C A R R   D A R E   R O I S T E R E D
R I O T S   F O R M   O N T   I R A
E N C H A N T S   A L L K E Y E D U P
  E R A   A B R A   S P A S
T H E B A B E   O S T E   A R C H E S
H I L O   B L O W H I S O W N H O R N
A R L O   E I R E   S A D A   E L I A
T E A M   D E E D   H U E Y   W E E P
```

#35

```
AMP  ALLS  LAMAR  STAB
GAR  POET  ANURA  ARCO
ORE  ARNE  REIGN  MARE
  PIRATE  GARYCOOPER
GRANTTINKER  LOMA
RARE  ELSA  SERE  TSE
ACERS  BETH  GOATY
MYSTIC  SAMUELBARBER
  CAVE  ONAIR  ALEE
 BUCKMINSTERFULLER
ERIA  PESCI  EENY
DENNISWEAVER  TRIBAL
DATES  IRED  ADORE
AKA  LASS  EAST  ELLA
  LEMA  MARSHAMASON
TINATURNER  HALEST
ACID  STEEL  ODEA  ERA
RENE  ERASE  REND  ROB
ODER  DELES  ERTE  STE
```

#36

```
DOIT  STAG  RAM  TOTAL
ONNA  TIME  IWO  AZURE
FENN  ALAN  GAR  FORTH
FROGINTHETHROAT  NIA
  CINDY  RETEST  PTER
TWEEDS  DOE  ELIHU
HENRI  LOUNGELIZARDS
YET  CLOGS  LAY  ASTEP
  STOOP  HES  RELAY
POST  SNAKEEYES  REDS
ALARM  TAX  HYPOS
CILIA  ACT  FERAL  CAY
TOADINTHEHOLE  IMAGE
  MONET  ORD  AVALON
STAR  LAHORE  ABELE
ARN  ALLIGATORWRENCH
BADEN  IND  EMMA  ADAM
OCEAN  DEE  LOOT  TARO
TERRA  SSN  LOFT  ERAS
```

#37

```
SATE  RAGES  CASTLED
ANITA  EBERT  ARCHIVE
ATEUP  PATRI  MARITAL
BIRDIBUSZIPPIBUS
  EARTH  SPAS  BILBO
SBA  RAE  LIED  SOON
TASTYUSSUPERSONICUS
AREA  ERIS  NATURE
GRAMM  GONE  TEDS  SGT
  EATIUSBIRDIUS
CCC  GULL  ASIS  SAGET
ORIGIN  PLEA  RITE
VELOCITUSDELECTIBUS
EMIL  CONY  SRA  BIT
READS  PICA  ATARI
  FAMISHUSFAMISHUS
ACTINIA  IDIOM  FAUST
BOOSTER  CIRRI  FALSE
ANTHONY  STEEN  CARP
```

#38

```
  CEDED  ABASH  RAJAH
ALLURES  RADIO  ABUSE
SUSANBANTHONY  FELIX
EMIL  ALAS  RELIT  IDE
APE  STEP  LADEN  MAES
  OLE  ALIBI  DREW
MAWKISH  INLET  ERASE
AVOID  ARMEE  ELBERTA
TOME  SWEAR  CREE  DES
TWA  BAKES  CORAL  HAT
HAN  ERIK  BATIK  ROME
ALSORAN  PUREE  TOWER
USUAL  SCARE  ROSTERS
  FRET  RINSE  RAH
ARFS  AGENT  LAIR  HOC
MAR  SPRAT  SILO  HERO
UKASE  AMELIABLOOMER
SEGUE  PERIL  AEOLIAN
EDENS  EDSEL  SPEND
```

#39

```
CARP  SWAT  MAIL  TIRE
ALAR  PARR  IRMA  HMAS
AGIO  ANTI  MISCREANT
 EDWARDSCISSORHANDS
GRILLE  KAY  OOT
AIN  GRATIN  BUS  RACE
RAGA  DRE  GAGS  ADOS
  MURDERINTHEFIRST
MASONITE  NAH  ANIMA
ASP  IGO  ANT  AOK  AIT
SHOAT  ERE  ALLIANCE
HOUSEOFSTRANGERS
ERST  PATE  CCI  HIRT
DEER  PRO  BRENDA  NEO
  ODO  ORO  ARAFAT
SUDDENLYLASTSUMMER
ERRONEOUS  TOMB  BRER
ADAM  NAME  IDEE  ENNA
LUBE  TMAN  COED  RODE
```

#40

```
 BAER  FIASCO  FATSOS
SELMA  UNCART  AGATHA
ADDEDINSULTTOINJURY
LEANIN  IMA  RTE  DES
  DIVIDEDHIGHWAY
CARS  ADEN  INS  SHEA
ARI  ODER  PEE  ACHARM
NATIVES  DISRATE  LEI
ABASE  TAL  TELLALIE
  ARITHMETICIAN
ENSWATHE  ASA  DOUAI
NEE  GLOBATE  AMONGST
DAMSEL  IVE  ASAN  LIB
SPIT  AGE  KNOT  OISE
  SUBTRACTEDFROM
ODO  ROI  RAF  ONEACT
MULTIPLICATIONTABLE
APIECE  RECORD  ARRAY
REDDER  KEYNES  PAIN
```

#41

#42

#43
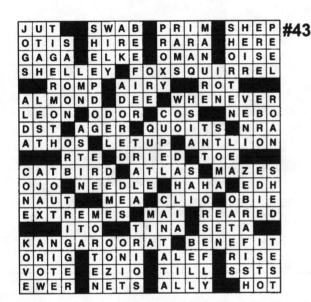

#44

#45

#46
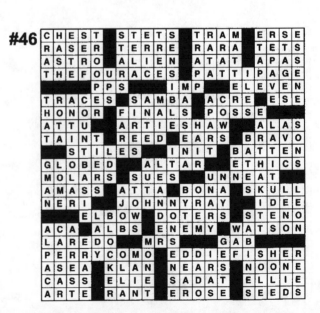

#47

```
ALA    HAUT   MATAS   POSH
MAXI   ROSSI  IMAGE   INTO
OPEN   IRKED  DATER   LION
   CONSIDERTHISBEFORE
BECHOSEN   PEEL    GENES
ONLINE    OAR   ARDOR
YOUMARRYFORMONEY    SCAM
ELBE   EARL    ROVER   OLE
RAS  STACY  STONE   ERNST
   TEACH  JOIN    ETUDES
 ITMIGHTTURNOUTTOBEA
ATHENS    HATE    SOULS
SWINE  MIENS   CUPID  JGS
TAN  REACT    THAI    SARI
ASEA  GREATDEALCHEAPER
 LOGES    IRE    ESTATE
COLTS    ARAN  SULTANAS
 IFYOUTOOKABANKLOAN
AFRO  RABID  GAUNT   IDEA
NEIN  ATONE  ETNAS   CITY
ORCA  SHEDS  ROKS     GEE
```

#48

```
CHASM   UPON   ARBOR    ABS
HYDRA   LARA   REUNE   SWAT
ADEAROCTOPUSFROMWHOSE
RES   IDES    NOUN    HELEN
    SPAR   REINS   OBOE
ALAMOS   WONT   ESTRANGED
SINUS   CHOO      ATE    LAY
TENTACLESWENEVERQUITE
ETA   SHALT  LIVER  UNDER
ROLF  IMP   CAGER  MITERS
   LSTS   HOTEL   TITI
SALONS   PERIL   PEA   LINE
TIARA   SLIGO   PARMA   LOS
ESCAPENORINYOURINMOST
ALE    LET     ONLY   IONIA
MERCILESS   IRES   SMEARS
   ONER   HARES   CHAS
ARGUS    ERIA   ERAT   TEC
HEARTSEVERQUITEWISHTO
ABET   ERODE   SLED  OHARA
BAL    CRESS   ALSO  NEWEL
```

#49

```
KASHA   EDENS   DOA   SMITH
ATTAR   NONNE   ENG   BASRA
FRANKFURTER   MANHATTAN
KING   ERIE   EMILIA   ALMS
APSE  REAR   NOSE   WALESA
   RAM   STARER    ALI
GERONIMO   UDO   TRIANGLE
ARENT   ANAPEST   AIN   AIR
PSI   HANDLE   EAST   DOGES
SENSEI   IAL   BOER   NAST
   ORLANDO   HILLARY
DOWD   SLED    ATV   TAXING
ILIAC   ASIF   THIRST   DEO
ELM   ISM   NITTANY   IDEAL
NAPOLEON   TOE   GARFIELD
   VIA   ATTIRE    AYN
DEFEAT   REEL   REST   GLIB
EMIR   ARCADE   ALEE   BORA
CONDUCTOR   TOSSEDSALAD
ATEUP   ESA   THEIR   STATE
YESES   SET   ESSES   ESSEN
```

#50

```
DELED    ARECAS    COSMOS
ERATO    BONHAM    ORIANA
FMURRAYABRAHAM   PETREL
EIRE   GOSSIP   ELI   AGRA
NNE   TAU   CEL   CENTRO
SEATO   NICOLASCAGE   TRA
ESTOP   GNU   SPAR   ASKEW
   EDEN   TRAM   ISNT  TILL
   DEEWALLACE   SALADE
AMI   OAK   BELLS   LINDAS
MIAMI   NERI   ISAW  IDEST
ARNOLD   SENSE   LIP   REY
 ACTORS   JOHNCAZALE
ACHE   SECO   ATOM   TICS
SLATE   NAIL    VIA  SHERE
PER   DIANNEWIEST   POLES
 LEADTO   GIS   RUS   EDS
ADEN   EEL   DOMAIN   ACRE
NOSTRA   ANJELICAHUSTON
AMORAL   BUNDLE   GEESE
TENETS   ASSETS   HADES
```

#51

```
 RAGS    ADELA   CLAMOR
PETREL   AGNOMEN   HAMATE
ATTIRE   BLYLEVENAMORED
STAFFAREA   ENE   ERIO
DORF   NODDY   DENTRANCED
ENSILES   DEA   OTO   HER
   NODE   EAR   JOES   NOLO
ABAFT   SANTE   END   CERES
SALAT   TECS   NNE   SAWERS
WHITEWASH   BOS   MERC
ENSURER   ALONE   OPPOSER
   AIDS   NIX   NOSTOMACH
CASTES   PTL   ARTA  OBLUE
ACHES   ERE   ABACI  LEASE
RUED   ENID   HOP   CHEW
ITE   MTA   AMT   IODIDES
BENCHARMED   BURST   TAVI
   OONA   RIP   RATPACKER
BRANCAPTIVATED   ASHORE
CATGUT   SEAGODS   DIETED
SETOSE   ESSEX     ADAS
```

#52

```
BBS    STEP   TAMP   AMAZE
LEHR   ATOLL  OXEA   RETAR
AROO   LAMIA  MINN   TARNS
HEWASCRAZYABOUTJULIET
SANDLOTS   ETON   OURS
   SARA   ODAY   AMMO   DRE
APSIS    POOL   NIN   ERIC
DAUGHTEROFLADYMACBETH
ITIN   ALOOF   SHOE  RODEO
OCT   PSI   LOON   SOL
SHEWASASHREWWEDTOIAGO
   HOE   CEES   EON   DES
STEEL   AARE   COSMO  SUNK
HETRIEDTOFRAMEOPHELIA
ARNE   OUT   AROW   OTTER
MIA   ALLY   OTTO   WANT
   SNIT   SPEW   TIMELESS
ROMEOCHOKEDHERTODEATH
ALAIN   OMEN   ELIHU  UVEA
TIZZY   ONIT   ESTER  PEAK
ADEEM   DINO   LEER    SKY
```

#53 · #54

#55 · #56

#57 · #58

#59

```
BOLT   CBER   AMAS   HOPETO
AMAH   ORSO   SOIL   OBOIST
HAVEANATTITUDE   ALLSET
SNARLS   CMON   ENROL
   ELUDE   PUTUPASQUAWK
EMP   ALEX   SNIP   NEUTRAL
BELLYACHE   DEEP   YENTA
BAIO   ROADS   SNERD   DIEU
INAWE   RUIN   DROOP   ERS
NINERS   STERE   AGAL
GETSOUTTHECRYINGTOWEL
   TSAR   RANON   OTTAVA
CAB   EVERS   SKEP   ISLET
EVAS   EYEON   TUXES   ORNE
DIMES   FLIC   MAKEAFUSS
ALBANIA   ACRO   COAL   SOT
RAISETHEROOF   TENOR
   NAIAD   TOMS   PHASER
STEAKS   WHINELIKEABABY
AWAKES   IONE   OVEN   IRAN
LAREDO   NEED   TENN   DANE
```

#60

```
ARTY   BEBOP   AFIRE   PREP
EERO   ALATE   RANIN   LANE
RHINOCEROS   GIANTPANDA
OOF   ATV   STCYR   DIRT
BULLFROG   SALEM   COOBAH
ASEA   INRE   MERITED   ABO
TERBIA   EARP   CASUALLY
   SNOWLEOPARD   CADET
PROJECT   CUOMO   MERE
LORICATE   TEMBLOR   ALE
AHAB   MENSA   MIAOU   TGIF
YEN   TERCETS   RONDELET
   GIRL   ITOUS   STAMENS
SAUDI   GRIZZLYBEAR
AUTISTIC   EYER   INAJAM
IRA   TITLIST   SIGN   LALA
CANARD   ETATS   METRICAL
GAEA   AREAS   MAC   UMT
SPERMWHALE   CHIMPANZEE
TREE   AERIE   KENAI   UZIS
YOKE   YMCAS   SANER   TINE
```

#61

```
LAMA   IGOR   ALAS   BRAWN
EXILE   RENE   MAMA   REGIA
ALLANJONES   ANON   ODETS
PENITENT   ANDREWWYETH
TSE   REEL   DIDO   ESE
   HARRYBELAFONTE   RAM
PECANS   ALS   LAS   ROLE
AVANT   TINA   KIDD   OBOE
GIRD   DANNYTHOMAS   GENT
ELL   PELTS   HANA   INURES
   REVILE   LON   STREET
PLEATS   GOER   STEED   ARM
LOIS   MARTINSHEEN   DLII
ANNE   MATS   ERRS   DIDNT
NEED   AIT   MAU   MIRAGE
ORR   EFREMZIMBALIST
   AIR   EELY   KANT   DOW
KIRKDOUGLAS   IDEALOGY
AMORE   TOIL   PETERFONDA
TENOR   ARNO   AGAR   FLEET
ETONS   HEAT   TOSS   LENT
```

#62

```
EGOS   DINA   HIRES   CAME
GOSH   SATIE   AVILA   URAL
GALA   ADLER   LOCAL   FALL
DONTWALKINFRONTOFME
   TOY   RAF   IRS
IMAYNOTFOLLOWDONT   PLO
HAN   GUAR   RHONE   PEEK
EDNAS   PIT   SCONE   NORMA
ARUM   WALKBEHINDMEIMAY
RELISH   LOOT   SAGER   STS
   DIOS   ADV   EWOK
ANT   LOTTO   OINK   ELANET
NOBELPRIZEWINNER   TELA
IVORY   ACORN   EER   TOGAS
SANE   VIAND   LIAR   RNS
EKE   NOTLEADWALKBESIDE
   MAI   AID   OVO
MEANDJUSTBEMYFRIEND
ONLY   EARLE   LIMIT   NOEL
COMB   RIGOR   DRIBS   DALE
APSE   SLEEP   SERS   SHAG
```

#63

```
ROMP   SAWED   ABBA   AHAB
ALAI   ALATE   BERRA   COME
MERE   RISES   ONEAL   TWIT
SOY   WITHSILVERBEL   DDE
MIO   RYE   IGLOO
PARRS   CUER   PIC   SLEPT
BUREAU   UPSILON   CAESAR
ANY   NEEDS   CAISSON   YSU
LIQUIDS   TRAP   ICED   OSS
SCULL   STAEL   ADA   CRUET
   IAL   ERRS   ACER   OAR
PATNA   NAT   VERSA   CIGAR
ROE   SEEM   WACO   BAKLAVA
ORC   DESPOIL   BASAL   RON
ATOMIC   LATERAL   REEDIT
MANIA   SET   TETE   ESKER
   TAMPA   OED   HEN
WAR   YTTERPDNASLLE   GOB
ELAL   ARTUR   ELLIE   TRUE
IMRE   HANSA   SAONE   HOST
RAYS   PATH   SNEER   EWES
```

#64

```
   SWIRL   ACCEPT   CLAIM
   STEVIE   ROOMIE   RIDGES
WHALEOFFORTUNE   AMOUNT
HELLS   TAUPE   NOPE   ATA
ARKS   SHINS   LOANS   SNAG
TEE   STAND   GOUGE   PEALE
SEDIMENT   CURSE   BULB
   WIND   TOLET   PERFECT
ALLOTS   SWELL   ALAS   ALI
BOONE   ROY   FEATURE   LOG
ACCT   EAGLERIGHTS   DOVE
TAU   ORIGAMI   ROO   LINER
ETS   PITY   PETES   WATERS
DETRACT   ERNIE   SACK
   HORA   SWEDE   BUCKAROO
SCOUT   CHESS   PUNKS   ERR
TAUT   LEURS   SANDY   FUEL
IRS   SOOT   PARKA   CONGO
FRIGID   OTTERCONFUSION
FINALE   FRINGE   CARSON
   EGGON   FUNNEL   EATEN
```

Crossword Puzzles

#65

```
SHIM  SERF  CAME  JASON
CORAM ONEI  ORAD  ERATO
AWARE LUNG  DOZE  RADIO
RADISHAROUNDSENSEBACK
CREOSOTE   ROLE    AMY
EDS  IRE  SERE  ANDY  CRT
  PAD  CHUG  TUT   SHEA
FEATHERSOPERASHOEHAIR
LUNA  UFO    OPT  ODESSA
IRA  DANO   FAIR  HILT
COLLARTRADERRACEFLESH
  YOUD  EGON   LADY  NIA
ARSENE SAL   SIN   LENT
CHESTNUTPLAYLATITUDES
HERS   SEE  DOIN   SRI
TAS  HEAR  TODD  AAA  MCI
  SUE   IOLE  ONACLOUD
POWERLAUGHFLYMACKEREL
OMARR  ISLA  LUNT  EVASE
LARVA  NEON  ELIO  RENTS
ANNOY  TROD  DEAL   ETAT
```

#66

```
LIBRA  SPARE  SHOP  CASA
ARIES  CANON  HOWL  HULL
HALFHEARTED  ALLY  ORAL
RNA  TERSE  EARL  ERICA
  TARRY    HAPPYGOLUCKY
LEEWAY  GLARE    ORBS
EARLY  RAIL  SPARTA  ORE
AVA  SHOVELS  IRES  GRAM
HELP  EDEN  COLON  RADIO
  ACRE    MADAM  SAFEST
FOOTLOOSEANDFANCYFREE
LISTED  PAINS    EASE
ALLOW  BUGLE  SAIL  SLOG
KEEN  FURL  ROTUNDA  AVE
ERR  HORNER  GARS  SEPAL
  FARM    OPERA  STALLS
DEVILMAYCARE    FLORA
EXILE  ARNO  OCEAN  NBA
BULL  ERLE  LIGHTMINDED
IDLE  PITA  OLLIE  SNEAD
TEAR  ADAM  GLENS  HERDS
```

#67

```
PANACHE   SPARTAN  ESPO
ABASHED   ASTORIA  STEP
WASHINGTONSQUARE  CALI
ESTE  ARN  TUN   SARTON
DEY  MARIES  EDIT  TOUTE
  RAGS  AHA  ENA  SWEAR
RECIPE  PLAZASUITE  OSS
APES  DEL  DUCTS  HALF
MINES  LENORE  EEE  ALAR
ACT  THEBOWERY  ASININE
DER  LEVER  ESSEN  BIP
ANATOLE  MANHATTAN  EMU
SELA  ESA  BOOHOO  SPRAT
  PEON  BEETS  UND  ETTE
OCA  WALLSTREET  OKAYED
CURSE  AEC  ERN  BOOR
ARKIN  DROP  STRUMS  SUN
RAWEST  RAP  ROY   ANNE
ITES  EASTSIDEWESTSIDE
NEST  SWEETER  RESIDED
ASTA  SEEDERS  SCENERY
```

#68

```
SRS  EMU  SWEAT  SRO  MEL
PIASTER  TALLY  TORTONI
LASCARS  ALLEN  ROBERTS
ALSO  GIANT  SEDUM  DART
STET  END    EMS   KLEE
HOSTS  EDDBYRNES  SNEER
  BIT  SEEDIER  ROI
DOSADOS  FESTA  CONGAS
ANTI  MITER  ATHOS  HIPS
NERO  BERRY  SHAVE  TROT
UNI  OSU    SEM   HUR
BEAK  STEAM  MOIRA  JOSE
ESTE  LARVA  ADDER  ALEE
  SENSES  ENATE  DIMMEST
  COY  DRIVELS  EPI
ARCUS  PATCORLEY  SEAMY
REAR  SOB    TON   FLOE
TINT  UNSER  DIANA  ALDA
INVITED  GAPED  DIARIES
SEASIDE  ARIEL  EVEREST
TDS  MER  NAPPY  REC  STY
```

#69

```
SHAH  ALEC    CARL  LABS
COMA  VIDAL  CAMEO  UVEA
ARAP  IFILOVEDYOU  CALI
RASP  ATE  LIRE   SKILL
PLAYERS  FLEETS  GABLES
  TRY  TRESS  HORNE
CLEAR  AWED  BARI  ASAP
HALL  SLOT  ALLEN  LANE
AMOK  COL  SKULL  PAINE
TAN  COHO  STREW  LADDER
  IOTAS  ARO  EMILY
DRIFTS  TITAN  DAME  CAW
RANEE  ASCAP  ARI  BOLA
OGRE  ALOON  SNIT  ELAN
PEEL  STUN  MICA  AWARD
  PETAL  ARETE  SRI
STEREO  SALOME  STATURE
LAVER   TITO  SPA  CHER
EMIT  WHEREORWHEN  HUGO
WITT  BENIN  YIELD  ERAS
SLAY  ALDA    GALS  DALE
```

#70

```
WAIF  RAVEL  GAGA   MALL
EDDA  EMILE  ATOP  HOSEA
BUYNOWPAYWAITER  ALTOS
SELFWILL   ITIS  GNEISS
  ANNE  FIDEL   GADS
STARED  NEVERABUMSTEER
AILED  DOLED   RIBOSOME
IRE  BIOL  AVALON   LEE
LOXSTOCKANDBAGEL  AIRS
TALE   OASIS   ADAGE
  DRABLY  HEMEN  CANINE
SOOTS   SAXON   OBOE
ATTS  BACHINTENMINUTES
LIT  REGENT   MOTE   ADA
AMERICAN   RAISE  PIGGY
DENOFANTIQUITY  TOSSES
  ALMA  RUNTS   SOIR
BADDIE  BAIO  UNUSABLE
AGAIN  SITEFORSOREEYES
GRIEG  ILET  SCARE  LESS
SASS  PERS  SAFER  ISTO
```

#71

RATA BESO BAR ASCARE
ALOP BANTU ADO KIOWAS
SORRYABOUTTHAT CRUISE
PETIOLES LIANAS OLLAS
CULL FOLIO PACED
MAJORS CLODS CONCEALS
ABUTS BOOKEMDANNO NEW
HISS DANO URGE MDVI
RET YOUARETHERE PACEM
ESTROGEN MEATY MOORES
HIKER KILLS BERRA
CREPES HALLE LIONIZED
LIFES AONEANDATWO YAR
AGAR SMOG ORTS IGGY
ROC UPUPANDAWAY ENURE
ARTINESS ARLES PREYER
SMITE AROAR SLID
EMMET SATCOM BIOCIDES
GOALIE WHOLOVESYABABY
EVADED LOS DAMAS LYON
REMASS SSE ETAL ESNE

#72

LAPP ARMOR ELISE PESO
ELUL PAINE LONER ARAM
TOREAPBRAVOSATLASCALA
SERAGLIO NINO OTTER
AYN DATES PLUS
STERN ARLO IRIS SAA
TOBEANOLYMPICMEDALIST
ATOM ANTES NAPES ELMO
BEN STEER INJUN IVAN
OAT DEUT GILA
TOSELLOUTCARNEGIEHALL
ORCS LEAH ORR
MART ASTRO SABER FAT
ATIE NITRO ALIEN PALO
TOBECOMEAMAJORLEAGUER
ORE ODER RAPS NANCY
SLED SPORE ENG
SIEPI SIAM OVERDRAW
TOWINANOSCAREVERYYEAR
ITER NOISE AMEND ETRE
RARE TREYS HUNTS SEEN

#73

LASSO PACA ASLEEP
CANTER ULAN LEARNED
FAITACCOMPLI BRISTLED
ASSERT APED DEBT RIFE
MESNE BHU WARIS DECAL
EDEN COUPDETAT TENACE
ZAIRE OLEG TALONED
CAF CARTEBLANCHE USS
OCASEY ELI SEMANAS
STIR CAME ETALII JOG
TORONTO EASTERN
ARE AEOLIS EMUS INGA
ABALONE LET APPEAR
MAU CAUSECELEBRE SNL
VISCOUS TION OUIDA
INCORP BONVIVANT RISK
VIRUS BORGE ECO MASON
AMIR PONE RASH MASQUE
SABATINI HAUTECOUTURE
LENIENT OGRE AUDIOS
STEREO DEAD PESCI

#74

THER STANCE FESTIVE
BRIDE IONIANS EMERSON
SINEW GRINNER RAPALLO
ENTRAIN LET TORI VETS
RDOF SABADILLA
ABCS ORAN TASS EIDOS
MULTILATERAL MANLIKE
ITEAS SHOE MOLARS ARP
STARTS INGW PING BNAI
SETTLES LEDUPTO RASA
REAP RULES INFO
ESTE MANTELS SNOUTED
PEEK ARNE DONE EXHALE
INA WISEST TAIN EAMON
CASCADE SPONSORSHIPS
STEAL OSAR OTTO ALEE
DENATURES OHAV
ACME OLOR SUE IDEALLY
COALHOD FREEMAN DIXIE
ENCLOSE SANDING ODIST
STEEPER STERNS NEIT

#75

ROT ACAD SCATS ECLAT
EPA TATI THEAIR LOINS
TENCENTS PAROLE ANGIE
ARIA TACH NINEMONTHS
GASTRIC OLEA SOLDAT
EIGHTBALL ILE CHEF
ANURAN RAN WAD ATOLL
SEVENYEARITCH EDD UVA
AVERT LIT HOI DEEPSIX
PEA ALL FUNT BLUES
FIVESTARGENERAL
PRIOR RIBO ELA STA
FOURWAY OTE HEM IMEAN
ALB AME THREEDOGNIGHT
CABIN OHS GAL IGNORE
TRES AMA TWOLEGGED
REATAS EINE OARSMEN
ONEMANBAND DRAW EOLA
GRETA LETTED BLASTOFF
ARCHI YEMENI CITE RIT
OAKEN NORSE SETA ENA

MAKE YOUR PUZZLE COLLECTION COMPLETE
with Simon & Schuster's Convenient Backlist Order Form

Now in its ninth decade of publication.

The Original Crossword Puzzle Series

——0-684-81473-0	#195	Feb. 97	Samson	$9.00
——0-684-86936-5	#218	Feb. 01	Samson	$9.00
——0-684-86937-3	#219	Apr. 01	Samson	$9.95
——0-684-86938-1	#220	Jun. 01	Samson	$9.95
——0-684-86941-1	#222	Oct. 01	Samson	$9.95
——0-7432-0537-5	#223	Dec. 01	Samson	$9.95
——0-7432-5096-6	#236	Feb. 04	Samson	$9.95
——0-7432-5111-3	#237	Apr. 04	Samson	$9.95
——0-7432-5112-1	#238	Jun. 04	Samson	$9.95
——0-7432-5121-0	#239	Aug. 04	Samson	$9.95
——0-7432-5122-9	#240	Oct. 04	Samson	$9.95
——0-7432-5123-7	#241	Dec. 04	Samson	$9.95
——0-7432-5124-5	#242	Feb. 05	Samson	$9.95
——0-7432-5125-3	#243	Apr. 05	Samson	$9.95
——0-7432-5126-1	#244	Jun. 05	Samson	$9.95
——0-7432-5127-X	#245	Aug. 05	Samson	$9.95
——0-7432-5128-8	#246	Oct. 05	Samson	$9.95
——0-7432-5129-6	#247	Dec. 05	Samson	$9.95

Simon & Schuster Crossword Treasuries

——0-684-84366-8	#40	Sept. 99	Samson	$9.00
——0-684-85637-9	S&S 75th Anniversary Vintage Crossword Treasury			
		Apr. 99	Farrar	$9.00
——0-7432-4795-7	#41	Nov. 03	Samson/Maleska	$10.00

Simon & Schuster Crostics

——0-671-87193-5	#111	July 94	Middleton	$8.00
——0-684-81380-7	#114	Nov. 95	Middleton	$8.00
——0-684-82963-0	#116	Nov. 96	Middleton	$8.00
——0-684-83652-1	#117	Aug. 97	Middleton	$8.00

Simon & Schuster Crostics Treasuries

——0-671-87221-4	#3	Mar. 94	Middleton	$8.00
——0-684-84354-4	#5	Mar. 98	Middleton	$9.00
——0-7432-0059-4	#6	Nov. 00	Middleton	$9.00

Simon & Schuster Fun with Crostics Series

——0-684-84277-7	#20	Jan. 98	Duerr	$8.00
——0-684-84361-7	#21	Jun. 98	Duerr	$8.00
——0-684-85942-4	#24	July 99	Duerr	$8.00

Simon & Schuster Super Crostics Books

——0-671-51132-7	#3	Mar. 95	Middleton	$10.00
——0-684-81340-8	#4	Mar. 97	Middleton	$10.00
——0-684-84364-1	#5	Mar. 99	Middleton	$10.00

Simon & Schuster Super Crossword Books

——0-671-79232-6	#7	Nov. 92	Maleska	$10.00
——0-671-89709-8	#8	Nov. 94	Maleska	$10.00
——0-684-82964-9	#9	Nov. 96	Maleska	$10.00
——0-684-84365-X	#10	Oct. 98	Samson	$10.00
——0-684-87186-6	#11	May 01	Samson	$10.00
——0-7432-5538-0	#12	Nov. 04	Samson/Maleska	$10.00

Simon & Schuster Large Type Crossword Puzzle Books

——0-684-81187-1	#1	Oct. 95	Maleska	$10.00
——0-684-84367-6	#3	Nov. 99	Maleska	$9.00

Savage Crossword Puzzle Series

——0-684-87195-5	#1	Jul. 00	Savage	$12.00
——0-684-87196-3	#2	Mar. 01	Savage	$12.00

S&S Super Crossword Puzzle Dictionary and Reference Book

——0-684-85696-4		Apr. 99		$15.00

SEND ORDERS TO:

**Simon & Schuster Inc.
Order Processing
Department**

**100 Front Street
Riverside, NJ 08075
Customer Service:
1-800-223-2336
Fax: 1-800-943-9831**

Total Cost of All Books Ordered _____

Add Applicable State Sales Tax _____

Check or Money Order Enclosed for _____

Please Charge VISA _____ MASTERCARD _____ AMEX _____

Card # _____ Exp. Date _____

Signature _____

Ship to:

Name _____

Address _____

City _____ State _____ Zip Code _____

PLEASE NOTE:
Prices subject to change without prior notice.
If any part of your order is out of stock when
we receive it, we will ship available titles and
will send a refund for the portion we cannot fill.

FIRESIDE
A Division of Simon & Schuster
A VIACOM COMPANY

Printed in the United States
By Bookmasters